THE ROAD TO DAMASCUS

LÉON STORK

Published by
Angela Blaydon Publishing Limited
2 Elm Close, Ripley, GU23 6LE
www.abpublishing.com

© Léon Stork 2008

ISBN: 978-0-9539821-2-7
EAN: 9780953982127

All rights reserved, no part of this publication may be reproduced, stored in a retrieval system, or transmitted in any form or by any means, elecgtronic, mechanical, photocopying, recording or otherwise, without the prior written permission of the Publishers.

Cover design and typesetting
© Angela Blaydon Publishing Limited

Cover photograph
Sunrise over the Sea of Galilee
© Léon Stork

Set in Times 12pt on 90gsm white uncoated Offset

Printed by Alden Group Limited, Windrush Park, Witney, Oxon OX29 0YG

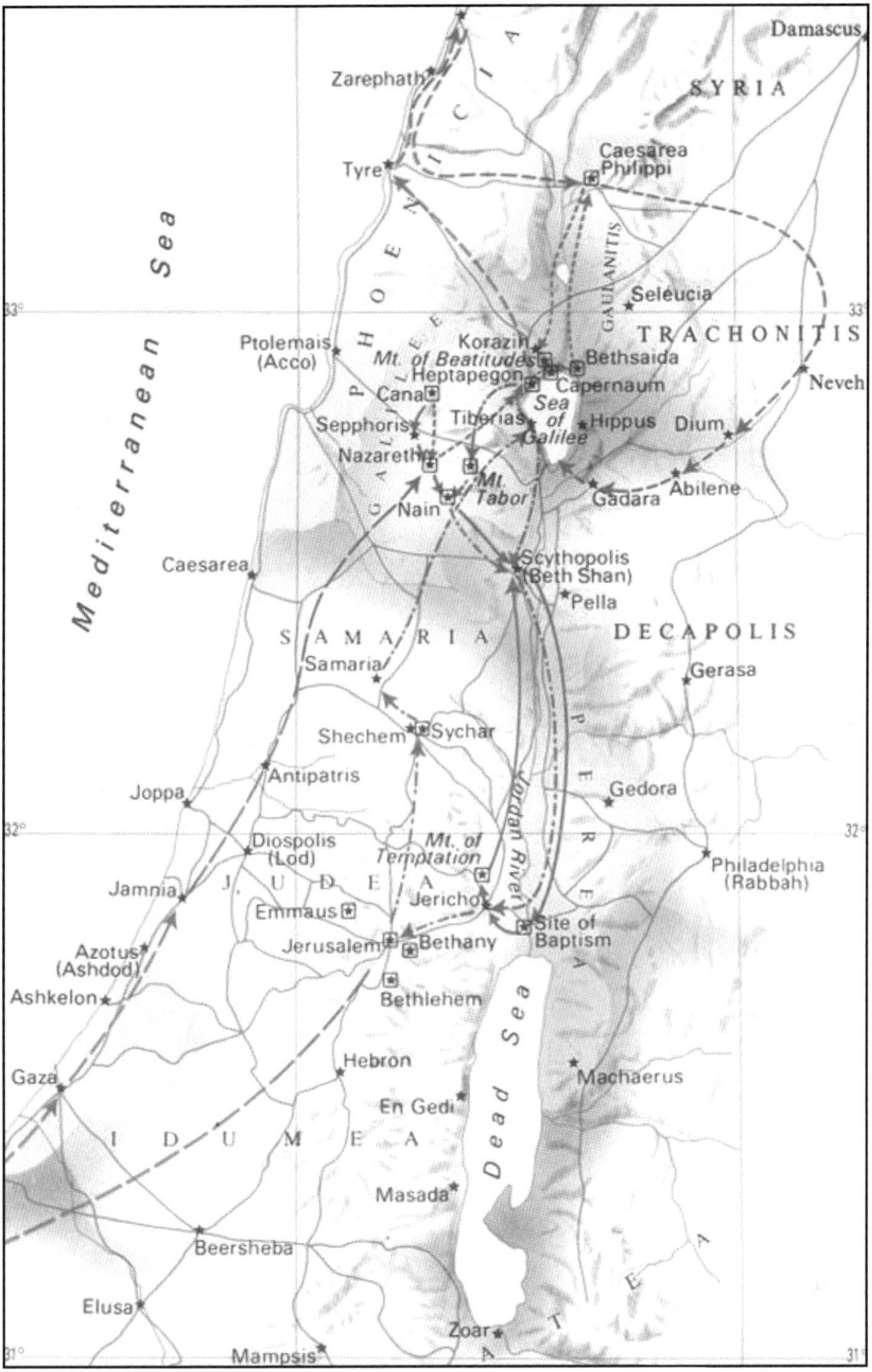
Damascus
SYRIA
Zarephath
Tyre
Caesarea Philippi
PHOENICIA
GAULANITIS
Mediterranean Sea
Seleucia
TRACHONITIS
Neveh
Ptolemais (Acco)
GALILEE
Mt. of Beatitudes
Korazin
Bethsaida
Heptapegon
Capernaum
Cana
Sea of Galilee
Tiberias
Hippus
Dium
Sepphoris
Nazareth
Mt. Tabor
Nain
Gadara
Abilene
Caesarea
Scythopolis (Beth Shan)
Pella
SAMARIA
DECAPOLIS
Samaria
Gerasa
Shechem
Sychar
Antipatris
Joppa
PEREA
Gedora
Jordan River
Diospolis (Lod)
Mt. of Temptation
Philadelphia (Rabbah)
Jamnia
JUDEA
Jericho
Emmaus
Site of Baptism
Jerusalem
Bethany
Azotus (Ashdod)
Ashkelon
Bethlehem
Dead Sea
Hebron
Gaza
En Gedi
Machaerus
IDUMEA
Masada
Beersheba
NABATEA
Elusa
Zoar
Mampsis
33°
32°
31°

**Facts support fresh
approach to Christian beliefs**
- author

PART ONE

covers Paul's journey to Damascus with details that are not mentioned by Luke or anywhere else in the Bible.

PART TWO

uses Paul's experience to confront problems he never encountered during his travels.

Preface

Newspaper headlines frequently warn us that the nations that occupy the regions bordering on Israel are inexorably hurtling towards a major conflict that will inevitably engulf the rest of the world.

If this happens, Israel, the original "favourites of the one God" could be involved in a war that would turn into their final Armageddon.

Christianity is powerfully linked to the oldest and largest religion mankind has ever known. But at a time when the world has never been amore affluent, the known word of God is being challenged as never before and the influence of Jesus and Paul is being degraded even by some of the most prominent religious leaders. From the tiniest nations to the most powerful country the world has ever known, governments and church leaders seem to be vying for the celebrity of being fraudulently authoritarian, selfishly destructive and brutally negligent when it comes to looking after the spiritual development of the peoples they are responsible for.

Can these sterile forces be arrested?
Can the Christians and the Muslims work out their differences and unite?
Can two wrongs make a right?

Christian leaders, with all the authority of representing the biggest and oldest religion, need to find the courage to eliminate the "impossible" elements that undermine their teachings and Faith. A new Covenant with God the Father is badly needed.

This will not only boost the spiritual integrity of the Easter message, its leaders would soon find themselves facing a massive open door beckoning them to say to all other religions to "come in and join us."

Part One

Chapter One

The coffee shop near the Aldwych is only half-full. Richard Clarke, a finance director with a city firm, sips thoughtfully on his cuppa as the fingers of his right hand drum impatiently on the table. His eyes flick up and down to the entrance where he expects his friend Jon Singer, a journalist, to appear.

The call from his friend was unexpected and badly timed. Richard has a number of tasks to complete before he disappears briefly on a private matter during the course of the afternoon.

Jon has become well known to those who read the tabloid for whom he works and his exposés of the high and mighty among politicians, celebrity aspirers and those whom his editor wishes him to bring to heel. His unpredictable schedules have made it difficult to regularly meet on a weekly basis with a group of close-knit friends.

In fact he is now known with affection as 'the outsider'. No one has quite given up the hope of converting him to become a Christian although the task grows bigger every day as his reputation as a slayer of big egos grows more eminent.

And now suddenly this invite for a coffee with a suggestion that it is urgent. What could Jon possibly want to discuss urgently with him? His eyes concentrate on his restless fingers and then suddenly another person sits down at his table.

"You're late," Richard says even before looking up, "I have to earn a living."

"I'll pay for your coffee," is the laconic offer.

"Gee thanks."

The two men, both approaching their mid thirties look quietly at one another. "What could possibly be so urgent? This meeting you and the others are going to this afternoon? Tell me about it." Silence as Richard studies his expression for any sign of mocking.

"We're all particularly interested in the Apostle Paul. I doubt if you have even heard of him. Unless you know something about him, listening to Ralph would be the equivalent of listening to a foreign language for the first time. He has some very interesting things to say about Paul. But he's not your average vicar, or whatever. I'm not going to tell you anymore about him because I do not want to stir your curiosity."

"Ralph who?"

"Just Ralph."

"Oh? A bit like Paul who was first known as Saul?"

"You have heard of him!"

"I was interested in religion during my first year, but it didn't make sense, just as nothing does if you look at what's happening in the world in the name of religion. I remembered you saying you planned to go to this meeting on Thursday? That's today."

"Yes today is Thursday. What do you want? Don't tell me you want to join us? What are you hoping to hear?"

Jon looks evasive and wonders for a moment if he can confide in his friend then changes his mind. "I can't tell you about it now. I just want to listen."

"The press is not welcome."

"I'll be there in a very private capacity." Jon is quiet, almost troubled. Richard is puzzled as he looks closely at the body language of the friend he has known since they were students at university. "You can come with me," he says hesitantly, "but I have to warn you, – and I want your solemn word, with no strings attached, you will not use anything you hear in any article you're writing today, tomorrow and or any other time. If you do you will find the group turning against you because in all probability Ralph will ban us from his church forever."

"Interesting. Is he a Christian?"

"He's a very private man."

"Then what's he doing in a Church?"

Silence, then Jon says cautiously: "O.K. I'm not coming to ask a lot of questions, or even one. I want to listen. Will there be a discussion afterwards?"

"Maybe, but only if any of us can think of something relevant to ask."

"I'm glad you take it all so seriously. That is exactly why I do want to sit in. I have a problem, and it is very private. You can trust me completely."

Richard takes a notebook from his folder and writes an address on a bit of paper.

"Three o'clock start at this address. It's a small church built with huge blocks of old stone. If you arrive from the wrong direction you won't be able to see it because of the large houses that obscure three sides of it. I'll warn Ralph you're coming. Strangers or unexpected visitors are not allowed, and there are perfectly normal reasons for this. We don't want idiots asking ridiculous questions. This is a meeting specially for individuals who are not part of any ministry anywhere, but who take their personal beliefs very seriously and who have problems with what is happening to the Christian church today, tomorrow and yesterday."

Jon nods and both rise and leave.

The short side road leading past the smallish stone built church is congested and a delivery van near the lychgate has to wait before reversing into a parking spot.

A 12-year-old boy, wearing a khaki lumber jacket and jeans, sits on the brick built wall separating the church garden from the road, resting with his chin on his pulled-up knees. His eyes widen slightly when he spots the van and the driver getting out, but he does not move.

The driver opens the backdoor and removes a trolley. He proceeds to pile four cases on to it. The church door opens and Ralph appears dressed in dark blue casual slacks and a short-sleeved shirt to match. Neither pay attention to the boy.

The driver unloads his trolley at the front door, nods his greeting and returns to the van to repeat the load. The boy watches intently as the man in blue signs for the delivery and then hands the driver a tip.

Before Ralph starts taking the load inside he walks down the path to the boy and asks, "Are you waiting for someone?" The boy quickly says "yes" expecting to be told to move on, but Ralph merely nods and walks back to the front door and starts to take the cases into the church. The van drives away.

Another hour elapses before a group of five young people, three men and two women aged around 30, gather at the lychgate where they are met by Richard and Jon Singer. The latter evokes surprise greetings from the others. There are handshakes and hugs before they slowly walk down the path to the front door.

Jon remains at the gate where the boy joins him. The others watch as he places a hand on the boy's shoulder and earnestly talks to him. Then the boy reclaims his seat on the wall and John joins the others going inside.

As he steps into the church he stops in his tracks. He had expected to see rows of pews but the hall is empty except for single pews moved against the two sidewalls. The entire floor is carpeted. At the front leading into the chancel there is a row of eight comfortable easy chairs near the uplifted pulpit. The walls are decorated with several murals, a couple of paintings and artefacts, which may be of a religious nature. To the right of the chancel there is a medium -size space separated by curtains from the main auditorium, and behind this a treadmill, a cycling machine, a weights machine and a punch bag are clearly visible.

He feels intrigued as he takes a seat next to Richard who immediately rises in response to Ralph arriving in front of them.

"This is Jon Singer, by nature an atheist and by inclination a journalist of some repute. Jon has always claimed he does not believe in anything for longer than a week or two but he has assured me, after insisting he wanted to come to the meeting, that he is not here as the Devil's Advocate."

All smile and Jon tries to do likewise.

Ralph is thoughtful then says to Jon: "You're welcome. There is only one rule at these meetings. No one is allowed to interrupt me. I speak off the cuff and if I am interrupted I will lose the thread and direction. I will in time answer all the questions any reasonably intelligent person may wish to ask me about the life of Paul – those bits we have a record of. And the bits you won't have heard of, you are expected to take my word for. If anyone is unhappy about this rule, then don't waste your time. Of course if anyone has a particular private difficulty then see me afterwards."

"I am told there is a restless air stirring among a group of young Christians, male and female". He pauses. "A resentment bordering on anger, looking to redress the balance weighing heavily against their faith in sections of the media. That's interesting, even though I do not intend to join the protests or whatever action you choose to take. Perhaps therefore it isn't inappropriate that we have a well known journalist with us today, and it may be interesting to hear afterwards if he wants to say anything to us to allay our fears about media conspiracy, or rumours that collectively they sometimes appear to be under the management and control of abominable forces. Or is it simply that most journalists, because of the nature of their work as creators of reputations, know exactly how shallow and trite their own assessments and judgements are? We all do what we feel we have to do under our own set of circumstances and we're always surprised, offended or even shocked if we are honest, by the way other people see us, sum us up, and then pigeon-hole us rather callously and ruthlessly."

"I am not accusing anyone here of suffering miss-apprehensions or illusions, but that just shows the power of the press." He looks at Jon. "You've got me talking about something totally different, which is unusual for me. I am not against free speech, which is why my meetings are only for those who believe in God. I don't have time to waste. I accept most British people are of a good nature, most of the time."

"You're here because you're curious to hear what I have to tell you about Paul," pausing slightly, "and I'll make up my mind as I go along how much I'm prepared to tell you".

"And it just so happens that I regard Paul as the most heroic Christian warrior in the Bible. He was one of us. The same definition cannot apply to Jesus because he was the original and without him we would never have heard of Saul, the Pharisee."

"Equally, it is probable that Christianity, without Paul, would have been known only as a small obscure sect confined to the religious and cultural traditions of the Jews and in opposition to it – one of the many on offer at that time in their history. There were many so-called prophets wandering about offering their own brand of god-worship and solutions to physical and mental problems – but all at a price."

"Paul's experience on the road to Damascus was surely the most significantly divine manifestation in the history of the world – that we know about. It was one of those occasions when everything about the Christian faith came together – the power, love and forgiving nature of God, the humanity of Jesus, and the spiritual hunger of Paul."

"God had to be in attendance himself to introduce Jesus to Paul to enable him to understand what was happening, and also because he alone controls everything connected with life and death, and because on such an occasion the powers of both the Spirit and human life were present."

"Paul experienced the indescribable ecstasy of being in the presence of the Creator, witnessed the miracle of the resurrection of Jesus, and was left afterwards with a full appreciation of the function of the Holy Spirit which Jesus first spoke about. He relied heavily on the presence of the Spirit to explain his message to the world afterwards. I think of Paul as the original Christian warrior, and perhaps even the only one ever, even though he never carried anything that could be remotely considered a weapon."

"On his travels he was confronted by just about every kind of danger, from the elements, wild beasts, and from two legged beasts who either tried to kill him, rob him or throw him into prison for preaching a message that made governments feel threatened."

"In reality he was probably the original back-packer, forced to working and walking his way around different lands, penniless at times, but refusing payment for his sermons. He was an amazing individual. The great news I have for all of you today, if you play your cards right, is that you could meet with Paul one day. Not quite in the way we have met today, but in a much more mind-blowing situation. More of that later."

"There are different ways to approach Paul whose speciality was the life hereafter. Although his letters dealt with the problems of his followers in various different countries, his message always concerned staying on course and maintaining a link with the next life."

"Some scholars are puzzled by the fact that Paul's sermons and letters contained so little information about the life of Jesus, despite the fact that Christianity is about Christ. It is also the story of Paul and his relationship with the God that introduced him to Jesus."

"As Paul matured into the role of being a very special apostle for God he once said: 'It is no longer I who live but it is Jesus who lives in me'. As the power of the spiritual union with the crucified Christ took over his days and his nights he began to understand more and more the power and control of the love of God. He has been criticised for not using Gospel material on his travels and in his sermons, but that was surely because Paul, through his Damascus Road experience, was convinced God had started preparing for the new world the Jews had been talking about for over a hundred years. Paul lived in the present and he became locked into the reality of the life of Jesus, his crucifixion and his resurrection. Added to this, there was the continuous confrontation with the followers and devout adherents of the Torah and its 613 laws and conditions. As a former Pharisee himself, Paul was very vigilant in the way he wanted nothing to distract from the real message of the Cross and life in the Spirit."

"He would travel any distance to establish communities whom he regaled with his most powerful message that life was continuous for those who deserve it. There was never any doubt in Paul's mind that an awful lot of people would not inherit life-hereafter and this presented a very challenging dilemma. With his Damascus experience came this deluge of a freedom he did not know existed, and at the same time he discovered that the freedom road was surrounded by minefields ready to blow the minds of those who attempted to put the cart before the horse. God loves you and if you follow Jesus your sins will be forgiven."

"But this was simply the preamble to later instructing his followers to in turn love and trust God and Jesus. All around him were uprooted and confused individuals. Israel was under Roman occupation. It was a time when lost souls were looking for religion. Much was on offer. The varieties were designed to please every nationality and tourist. Some claimed they alone could solve the riddles of life and others encouraged individuals to indulge in Eastern techniques aimed at achieving a spiritual state. Competition was rife for miracle workers and preachers claiming extraordinary results. All tastes were catered for, at a price."

"Paul offered knowledge of the way to the only God, and it was free. He always turned down offers of money, although when he spent time in prison, probably because his fiery personality caused disturbances, he allowed friends to send him food. And for the thinkers his sermons about a forgiving God and his crucified son held much appeal."

"He had extraordinary courage, determination and commitment. He always managed to capture the attention of listeners with his wonderful revelation of what it was like to be in the presence of God. He stood as a monument of God's love and forgiving nature, but he knew he had to live up to his own expectations because more than anything else Paul wanted to make sure he would, when his time was up, return to the presence of God."

"He knew there was no way he could stand before his Maker and exclaim, 'Here I am God! This is who I am, this is how you made me, this is what I became, you must take me as I am.' Such arrogance and contempt never became part of his character. He always gave God all the credit for the success of his missions. Paul always thought he had to redeem his earlier life, and that he would be judged by the legacy of the Christian communities he had established. For that reason he kept in touch with them, and the subsequent doubts, failures and the threats of those who deliberately tried to undermine his work on a previous visit."

"With the freedom that Paul preached, came understanding of what a monster he was before the Damascus experience. He had used his misguided intelligent strength to argue with the fragile minds of uneducated Jews, and subsequently stood by to witness their physical torture and incarceration by the law, the police or the Romans."

"Paul found it difficult to understand why his own people, the Jews, found it so difficult to appreciate the good news he brought. He saw himself as testimony to the existence of the one true God and he felt that he was living proof that Jesus was alive and well."

"And so Paul became the cosmopolitan Gentile, often on the run from those Jews who wanted to kill him for daring to dismiss the laws of the Torah and the traditional Jewish lifestyle. They would not accept that there was fault in the 613 laws of the Torah and the damnation they preached would follow if any individual broke one of these. When he pointed out that the Torah laws lacked the humanity of Jesus, he was called a traitor. It was tough for the man who would never concede defeat to the misguided and often warped free wills of others. He offered the only solution for those who looked for the meaning of life. He wanted to free his fellow men and women from the shackles of certain death. The grace of God was available to one and all, but he also warned, those who did not search for God in this life, did not have a hope in hell of finding him in the next."

"Paul never lost his enthusiasm for the task he had set himself because he never lost touch with the Damascus Experience. He never lost his gratitude for the God who had overlooked what he was before his redemption put him on the right track."

"His many journeys to countries to the north of Judea did not become easier. It was one thing to regale listeners with what it was like to be in the presence of God, it was another thing to overcome the arrogance, deceit, vanity, indolence, self-satisfaction, criminality, of free wills battling with the complexities and absurdities of every day life."

"All religions believing in an after-life of sorts had laws for adherents to follow to earn the riches and wealth that their particular messages promise with their god. The Damascus Experience enabled Paul to work backwards from his experience in the presence of his Creator. If he lived today he would surely have altered his choice of words many times. Some of the things he claimed at that time are simply unacceptable to us today."

"There are many things about life and the way some people die that still puzzle us. The reality of the Damascus Experience often still eludes us.

"God wants us back, but not everyone will make it. Such is the power of God; He becomes immediately available at the death of every individual. There is no time wasted in between. Contact has to be maintained. Judgement is immediate and the simplicity with which it is delivered is the ultimate Truth for every individual – if contact is lost that is it. No one has ever seen what happens when contact is lost, but any existence away from God, after a taste of what it would have been like to remain in his presence, has to be grim in the very extreme. There is no second chance."

"Next time any of you find life upsetting, too challenging or simply not worth the effort, think of Paul on his travels suffering from hunger, being shipwrecked, in prison, threatened by wild animals and people, and still pursuing his aim to find new people to tell the wonderful news that God exists, Jesus is alive, and that the freedom that accompanies such belief belongs to every individual."

"Paul never talked and wrote about wars and such like. He was totally pre-occupied with the latter stages of the life of Jesus, with his own Damascus experience, and with the wonderful news that there is nothing on this earth that can remotely compare with a loving and trusting a forgiving God. From birth every individual is born with the trust and knowledge that one day they will return to the presence of God. That is what He wants and that is the purpose of creation. The catch is that there is a requisite. Every individual has to love God and want to return. That Love cannot be switched on like a light bulb. That is the righteousness of the Father."

Ralph pauses and looks towards the gym, his hands resting on his hips.

A man's voice says: "But Paul did retaliate when Torah Jews visited his communities to tell people he was not a proper apostle and that he was enticing Jews and Gentiles to break traditional laws."

Ralph turns to face Peter who continues: "He wrote letters. You may well ask what good would that be today? We are constantly besieged by atheists who dominate the media, television channels and some newspapers. What about the time when Jesus physically removed a gang of traders selling their wares in a temple?"

Peter sounds troubled and gets to his feet, watched closely by the others.

"When my mother died, father just sat there with anger burning inside him as he looked at her lying lifeless on a slab. Her piety had controlled his barbaric heart all their married life and he had always resented it. As he looked at her he said he saw nothing in her expression that indicated a better place wherever she was. His instincts told him she was dead and that everything was futile despite all her claims about good and bad and that the bad would be punished by her God."

"I had to choose between being like her or like him and I chose her. But here I am burning with resentment because of all these bastards who besmirch our television screens and newspapers with vile obscenities. And they do it all in the name of freedom. Why can't we retaliate? I feel like sinking my fist into the face of so many men and women now that we're all equal – especially political activists. And it's getting worse month by month. We have a government that despises traditional values and Paul himself has been unpopular with church authorities for many years. They don't understand him because they have created a kind of Christianity that at best is a political way of life. God's presence is being squeezed out of religion in favour of the promoters of a new UK, and a new political philosophy giving the next generation the green light to believe booze, drugs and one parent families are as acceptable as what used to be known as traditional family life."

He pauses for a few seconds then continues: "I'm here because I'm still looking for some sign somewhere telling me mum is OK. I am looking forward to you saying that you despise the hate producers and writers as much as I do. Turning the other cheek today is the wrong message. We're being steamrolled underground because of the weak leadership in politics as well as religion. Surely this has to be one of the most destructive times in the history of the world's psyche as small groups of outsiders, clamouring for identity and status as well as lottery support, get it. Kids in school are being taught it's acceptable to be one of them. What chance has Christianity got to survive when only the bullies, and especially the very destructive ones appear to be in charge, boosted by ridiculous laws in the guise of human rights. Exactly what sort of yob culture are they striving to impose on this once great country?"

Ralph chuckles. "You really are confused. There is nothing more powerful than the messages from Jesus and Paul. They complement one another perfectly. You're right to claim that the Church as an institution appears to be drifting away from its original roots in exchange for sophistication. Without exception, all God's enemies aim their destructive tactics against the nature of the invisible Christian God. They see that as his Achilles heel. We both know they can't succeed. But we have to get on track with the real Christian message."

Peter is unable to contain himself: "Hooray, you are on our side!"

Then he reclaims his seat and mumbles: "Sorry I did not mean to interrupt, but it's just so stupid. We can all see what's going wrong, and what needs to be done. Why is there no political will to do this? Why do we allow such lies to be spread by the media? Why are the greater majority of journalist's atheists? None of us present want to be part of a kind of freedom without truth, without morality, without Christian commonsense and without the God of Jesus and Paul."

Silence, then Ralph says quietly: "Paul had the same problems. As soon as he was away from the newly established Christian communities, there were always elements trying to breach the barriers of the new freedom. Paul went to great pains to explain there was no point in replacing the Torah laws with just another set of laws."

"But Paul's eruption of joy when he understood that the Damascus experience had brought with it the news his own sins had been forgiven was something Christians must never lose track of. Paul never lost touch with this. It gave him the insight to appreciate that continuous life really did depend on living in the Spirit. It did not detract from the truth that all people still had to earn a living but it gave them a new perspective on the lives they should live among fellow men and women."

"He understood clearly that anyone not in touch with life in the Spirit would be very vulnerable to all the nasty challenges and temptations of life. It would cause them to make unacceptable judgements about their own lives, and those of others they were in contact with on a daily basis. It would send them careering in wrong directions, and their deeds would destroy the sensitivity of their own minds and this would prevent them from entering the Kingdom of God."

"There are ways to unify the worlds two largest religions were it not for the leaders of these two religions."

He stops and Jon waits expectantly, then asks: "The suspense is killing me. I hope you're not worried about my presence. Please ignore it. Nothing you say today will be used by me at any time without your permission and then, I promise, I will allow you to check my copy to ensure I got it right."

Ralph smiles: "You have the body language of a man on a mission."

The reply is immediate: "I am on a mission yes, but writing about this meeting is not on the agenda. Maybe at some time in the future writing about you would be my honour and challenge. I can see why you're concerned, but you need not be."

Ralph says curtly: "What about the boy on the wall outside?"

Jon nods. "He's a little friend from Palestine visiting the UK with his father."

Ralph turns to the others who have listened intently.

"There is a kitchen at the back, and a bottle of dry white wine on the table. I'll have a mug of coffee if anyone decides to make some."

The two women rise, followed by the men and leave.

Jon remains behind and asks hesitantly: "I am told you are not an ordained priest?"

Ralph nods: "No. Living like this is an experiment. When this church became redundant I bought it and here I am living in it."

"Why are you an expert on Paul?"

"I would not claim that. But perhaps if you studied him as closely as I have you might discover a bonus for yourself."

"Are you simply on an individual pilgrimage to convert as many people to Christianity as you can?"

"I would not claim that either. I am simply prepared to share my knowledge with those who want to listen. I do not convert, I merely explain life has different roads to choose from, and each individual owes it to himself to weigh his options with great care. Ultimately the choice is yours alone."

"I was told this is not a discussion group."

"What I say is not up for discussion. That is why it is an experiment. Is your young friend looking for religious instruction?"

"He is not aware of it yet."

"You're looking on his behalf? But you're an atheist?"

"His father is a Muslim fanatic."

"Ah? You have spotted a journalistic challenge? Does he attend a school?"

"He did in Palestine, a very good school but he's only been in the UK for a couple of weeks. He's almost 13 and he's been through a lot, but he does speak and write English well. I think you may be the man I'm looking for. Your message seems to be non-ecumenical even though Jesus and Paul feature strongly."

"He's a good listener and he asks surprisingly intelligent questions coming from his sort of background."

"I'll think about it."

Jon looks relieved. "Does that mean I can come and listen to you again?"

Ralph nods: "You're unusual. You're not so much interested in your own spiritual redemption as that of a young boy. That's a move in the right direction."

Jon's reply has a terse ring. "What sort of people do you consider are beyond redemption?"

Ralph smiles. "Are you thinking of the man crucified next to Jesus? Very late redemptions must be tricky. I would say it depends on the state of mind of the individual. The man crucified with Jesus is not known. I have a feeling that in our courts of justice, the case against him might have been thrown out of court. There are those who live such extraordinary lives they never remotely touch base with either God or Jesus. They seem to studiously obey the laws of the land but somehow make sure they are deprived of knowing what humanity is all about."

"What about the other forms of religion?"

"It would depend on their perception of God, how they live their lives in relation to other people and how they differentiate between good and evil. I am not interested in religions. I support wholeheartedly what I know about Jesus, but not necessarily Christianity as it is preached in some churches today. In the meetings we are having I concentrate on Paul, and his crucial role in explaining to everyone prepared to listen what sort of God we worship. And he particularly concentrates on what happens when we have to abandon our bodies."

"Make no mistake about it. God wants everyone back, for however brief a period. We don't know what his reasons are for taking us back, but if we consider how difficult he has made it for himself by giving every new baby a free will to grow and develop into a massive potential enemy then it conjures an extraordinary wonderful picture of his joy to welcome back every new arrival with the proper credentials to inherit continuous life. You'll be amazed how many intelligent humans are prepared to challenge their creator with the demand: 'This is me God, this is how I was born and chose to live my life, this is where I'm heading, this is what I give to charitable causes and this is how you must accept me. Surely that is what Christianity is all about. If I am selfish, that is how I was born?'"

"This is what Paul was afraid of for his converts and he was criticised for giving the impression he was a tough teacher who thought he was always right. During those times he probably was. Don't forget, everything we know about God is what we learnt from Jesus and Paul. I sympathise with what I heard from Peter tonight, but next time any of you feel like throwing a punch, come and see me. I have a bag you can hit as hard as you want to."

All look at the gym equipment.

"And if that isn't enough, think about Paul's experience on the Damascus Road and then try facing up to God and asking him if it's OK to resort to violence. No one has a hope in hell of getting within a million miles of his Creator if his mind and heart does not support his desire."

Elizabeth says gently, "Everything you say sounds intensely personal. Do you first assess your audience before you decide how much or how little you will tell and how long do you need to decide what to say? Are there any personal aspects of your faith and your own experiences that you don't talk about?"

Ralph smiles. "I have no difficulty in talking straight to you. Everything I have said is highly personal and everything I might add next time will be in the same vein."

Jon attempts to sound light hearted – a skill he hasn't yet mastered properly: "So you don't really think very late last-second redemptions are possible without the matter having being seriously discussed and considered beforehand?"

All rise from their easy chairs and contemplate Jon's question. When Ralph makes no attempt to reply Elizabeth laughingly interjects: "Well that's the first time I have ever heard you use words that imply you might be on the same planet as us, Jonny? You're always so intent to exact your sort of justice through your articles. Does that mean there may be an awakening taking place in your brain, your mind, or perhaps even your conscience?" Her smile indicates an intended humour but she does not expect a reply and does not get it.

Chapter Two

Two days later. It is just after 8 am and Jon Singer carefully parks his Golf near the lychgate leading into the churchyard. It has been a hectic 36 hours since the news hit the headlines in every newspaper about the police raid and shoot-out at a North London address, leading to the death of two suspected terrorists.

No names have been released and there has been huge speculation about the arrests, whether they were illegal immigrants, or residents with British passports.

But that was the least of Jon's problems. For once he did not care about getting the full facts of the story before any of the other papers. He remains seated in his car for a couple of minutes before assembling the courage to get out and slowly walk along the path to the front door.

A light towards the back end of the church indicates life and he moves around the side of the building to see of there is a side entrance. When he finds it, his hand reaches for the knocker and bangs gently twice.

Almost immediately the door opens and Ralph looks at him with surprise.

"I do apologise...." Jon begins but is interrupted.

"Come inside."

He is led into the kitchen where Ralph looks at him expectantly.

Jon seems nervous and unsure of how to start. "I've lost the boy. He seems to have disappeared."

"And you think he might be here with me?"

Jon immediately shakes his head and hesitates. "I'm afraid he may have been involved, as a victim of what happened in North London. I expect you've read or heard the news? He doesn't answer his mobile, and that is bad news. I gave it to him and it was the greatest gift he's ever had.

It provided him with a new kind of identity. I did leave a rather presumptuous message on it, in case he is able to use it."

Ralph waits expectantly. Jon continues: "I said if he felt he was in trouble to head for this church and to contact me through you. I hadn't heard from you and I thought I should drop in and warn you of what may happen."

"Are you saying the police are looking for him?"

With his eyes fixed on Ralph, Jon says slowly, "No – his own people will be. Not all those who were in the North London house were taken into custody. Some managed to get away."

Ralph's tone is demanding: "Are they terrorists?"

"Suspected terrorists are what journalists were told by the police. Raf's father was visiting a friend at this address before the start of the raid."

"How do you know that?"

"I had spoken to Raf earlier and he told me he was on his own, his father not having returned from a visit to this friend in North London. His father also has a mobile but he hasn't been in touch since, which is just as worrying."

"What about his mother."

"She was killed by a bomb back in Palestine."

"What is your connection with this boy?"

"I met him in Palestine while covering a story of the conflict there against Israel. He has an almost ethereal quality about him and he surely takes after the mother I never met. But he has been under his father's control and performed many tasks you wouldn't approve of."

"And ……?"

Ralph waits expectantly. Jon's voice lowers in tone: "I interviewed them as a family. His father has the air of a man who could be involved in anything and everything. When I asked the off-the-cuff question whether he had ever considered moving to the UK the father jumped at it as though I had made them an offer. He would not leave me alone after that whenever I saw him again and the idea grew on me. The boy seemed so out of place with what was happening in that part of Palestine. I saw it as a chance to help and also to get a great story."

He hesitates, looking unsure of himself then asks: "In all the time I have known them I have never once seen the boy smile. What are your feelings about the situation in Palestine?"

Ralph is thoughtful. "The leaders of both countries need to show they are prepared to talk. So much of what is happening over there seems to be from another world and lifetime. The relentless presence of such a war is very oppressive and soul destroying for the people who live there. It is monstrous environment for children like Raf. I am not interested in the politics of what is going on. My interest is to help individuals in a different way. Although I sometimes have groups over here for my talks on Paul, I mostly concentrate on historical matters on those occasions. I am only willing and prepared to help when it does not compromise my personal position as a law-abiding UK citizen. I have no desire to become involved in terrorist activities or mob cultures."

Jon adds thoughtfully: "So you really have no opinion on war? The same as Paul, because you mentioned that he never spoke about it. All the Palestinians I spoke to are reconciled to the fate of having to fight to the death in an all or nothing situation. The only judgement they seem to understand is their need to push Israel into the sea. Turning the other cheek is not an option or Muslim virtue."

"What is your involvement with what is happening with this boy? You cannot and must not take this building and me for granted. If you do I will have to take measures to prevent you from doing that. We're almost strangers and I don't trust your motives. What did you have in mind when you asked the boy to come to this church and make contact through me?"

"Isn't the church supposed to be a place of refuge for people in trouble?"

Ralph scrutinises his expression closely before saying: "Suddenly you're not an atheist anymore?"

Jon's reply is swift: "I wasn't born an idiot. I may not believe in the afterlife you specialise in, but I'm not anti showing kindness where I deem it to be appropriate. Churches are known to do some good charitable work among the poor and deprived."

Ralph interrupts: "Well now you know this is not a traditional church. It is a redundant church with no links at all with traditional religion. And I have the right to ask you a few relevant questions, since you are attempting to draw this building and its owner into a highly suspicious activity. Did you have any knowledge of what Raf's father was up to, and why he wanted to come to the UK?"

"No," is the immediate reply, "although I suspected there was a connection with terrorists, I concluded it was no more than almost everyone who lives in that part of the world. It is part of daily life, and this man, Raf's father, was struggling to make a living. Raf seemed to be drifting inexorably into the mire deeper and deeper."

Ralph sounds suspicious: "And it touched you so much you decided to risk your job and your own freedom helping them sneak through Customs?"

"As a journalist I thought I could get away with it, if the worst came to the worst, by claiming to be doing it as a test to see how alert Customs are at the ports," Jon says quickly, before adding thoughtfully, "I did not really have much time to contemplate the consequences. It was the boy that prompted me to suggest, almost as a joke, that they might do better living in the UK. The father was so taken with the suggestion he would not leave me alone after that. At that stage there was never the slightest suggestion that he knew people in the UK until after we had driven through Customs and were heading for London."

Ralph lowers his voice: "And now you feel you are responsible for this boy? It could be for the rest of your life? And just turning up with him at your flat could cause all sorts of very awkward questions. So suddenly you're not the great big 'shoot from the hip' atheist after-all?"

Jon looks sharply at him to see if he was being mocked.

Ralph continues: "You're overlooking the fact, if that is what you're hoping to hear me say, that having that boy living here would provide me with exactly the same sort of difficulties. I cannot and will not be seen having a young boy living here with me."

Jon turns away and measures his reply carefully: "I don't know any place I can risk taking him – it shouldn't be longer than for one or two nights only. He trusts me, and I cannot abandon him. I have no clear idea yet what sort of trouble he and I are in. The police will not reveal the names of those two killed and the three in custody. All we have been told is that some, perhaps as many as four, managed to get away. It is quite possible they don't know. Raf seems remarkably calm considering his predicament, but I have not discussed this in detail with him. I admit I feel out of my depth if this boy starts telling me things I do not wish to hear. But listening to you gave me a bit of hope"

"Perhaps the real reason why I am here talking to you, is because I heard you say that you could see, or you hope to see a time when the Christians and Muslims might unite in worshipping the same God. I don't understand or appreciate what you meant, and whether you actually think you know how this could happen, or is it just pie in the sky stuff. I think Raf might be interested in listening to you"

Ralph sounds surprised: "Am I right thinking that you're looking for a miracle to get you out of this? Without apparently knowing anything at all about the character or expectations this boy may be harbouring? There must be a good chance he could be a Muslim fanatic, even at his age, and you want me to try and convert him?"

For the first time Jon sounds almost apologetic: "I have never heard him say anything to suggest he might be a terrorist, except he does claim to be here working for Allah." He takes a deep breath before adding: "Although some might claim that sounds like a war cry, I have found my relationship with Raf comfortable and reassuring."

Ralph is not convinced: "That may be because you haven't yet asked him your usual penetrating questions? So we don't know how much indoctrination he has had to endure in his young life."

Eagerly: "I know he went to a good school. His father was proud of that."

"And you obviously believed him, despite knowing he was street trader who make a living from outwitting tourists." He pauses before continuing. "I can't quite make up my mind whether you're simply playing journalistic games with your two visitors or whether deep down you guessed there might be problems, but that it could work out very well for another scoop. Or are you saying deep down in your own barbaric heart there might be a dark corner desperate for some light to shine in?"

Jon steps away, stops and turns: "I admit initially I was attracted by the story, and by the challenge of bringing father and son through the porous Customs system into the country. Now that that has been achieved, and after what happened last night I feel out of my depth. If you can't and won't help I'll accept that."

"I don't belong to any church but I do believe you can help this boy far better than I can. Believe it or not, I do try to stick to facts as closely as I can."

Ralph says smoothly: "The most successful conmen are those who stick as closely to the truth as they dare and sometimes, like others in your profession, when the facts don't help you simply alter them with a different choice of words. Perhaps you're on the way to finding out that without truth there can be no meaning."

The two men look silently at one another before Jon says: "I know you have no reason to trust me but my fear for this boy is genuine."

"Why don't you go to the police?"

"The reasons should be obvious to you."

Ralph is direct: "And you want to know if you can trust me? Do you appreciate I could end up behind bars. I am not ordained, so I have no standing, no back-up protection. Even so, you presumed you could trust me when terrorism is the biggest threat to world peace."

He looks accusingly at Jon who seems to be in trouble looking for a reply. "I came to see you and to listen to you before the events of last night. And that wasn't because I was looking for a story – a new breed of Christian seems to be emerging and it wants to fight tooth and nail for its roots and beliefs. That is why my friends are here; in the hope you will become a leader. I felt a suspicion you may be able to help me save this boy. I admit, I am here today because I know of no other place to go."

Ralph nods: "But now things have taken a decisive course – the shoot-out last night. You think the boy's father was involved and you don't know if he is still alive. If he isn't, why should anyone else be interested in the boy, unless it's a relation or a friend? What on earth do you expect me to be able to do to help?"

"I feel you're the only one I can trust. All my friends trust you. You don't sound as though you're hung up on day-to-day politics so you won't be breaking convention or Church rules or laws, whatever they are. You're a real independent. I have nowhere else to go."

Pause before Ralph says softly: "Terrorists are guilty of spreading the message of hate and they're using their extreme religious views to recruit young minds."

Jon, nervously: "But you think you can see ways of uniting the two religions. Christianity sounds like the opposite. Even I might be tempted if I could accept the existence of palaces and a Rolls Royce in the sky."

Neither feels like smiling. Again Ralph closely studies his edgy body language: "It must be quite a job to reason with you. You're probably at your most productive when asking questions and jotting down answers. I'm not even sure where you're coming from. I only briefly mentioned the possibility of the two religions worshipping side by side. It could take a hundred years to achieve and even then it could only happen if both sides knocked down what looks at this moment like extremely fortified stonewalls. If only they could accept that Paul's story tells them how to do it."

Jon sounds hopeful: "My friends like to listen to you. They keep coming back for more. That's a position of strength. Even I am here for that same reason, although you know it's not the only reason. From what I heard you say earlier God isn't interested in my problem, so falling down on my knees and praying is not going to help because time is not on the side of prayer. From what I know about the two religions there is no hope of uniting. Muslims see Christians as the enemy. The Christians that Peter want to beat up are probably the ones that might agree with unification, but for different reasons. The other Christians probably feel the same way as the militant Muslims."

Ralph's says deliberately: "The papers say the shoot-out was between suspected illegal immigrants and the police. Do you think that is a possibility – rather than a battle against terrorists might be looming?"

Jon takes so long to reply that Ralph adds: "You must have your own suspicions? How do you read what has happened?"

Jon's drawn facial expression exudes concern as he says: "I have felt suspicious ever since we drove through the Channel – a chance light hearted remark by the father that a bomb in the tunnel might do a large amount of damage if it was big enough. It was the fact that he was thinking about the size of the bomb rather than the fact that disturbed me. Raf made no comment at the time. He has never said anything that worried me. I recall wracking my brain before our meeting in Paris for any sign or misplaced word, but there was nothing. Perhaps my enthusiasm and excitement at helping them clouded my judgement. He was always just the boy doing what his father asked him to do."

Ralph pours water into a kettle. "I'm having some coffee. Will you join me?"

Jon nods as Ralph says: "Is there anything else you can recall?"

"Very soon after their arrival in London I began to lose touch with the father but I became closer friends with Raf and I began to have my suspicions that I had been taken in by the father who wanted to make contact with a group of refugees or immigrants, perhaps illegal like him. I made up my mind to concentrate on Raf and to do what I can to help him. Fortunately he had a place to stay. I was contemplating drawing in the two women who were here listening to you but now the business of last night made me decide to trust you instead. I have dropped plans to write about smuggling them into the country. I now know that if my suspicions are corroborated I would lose my job and could find myself behind bars. A week ago the boy told me his father was in serious financial trouble and that is why he was so keen to come to London to link up with friends."

"A story I wrote a week ago gave me the chance to help. It was about the love life of a prominent politician, and I received a tip about photographs pinned to the door inside his bedroom wardrobe. I remember the agility of Raf in the Gaza strip squeezing through windows while looking for something to eat in the rooms of tourists. I took him to the home of this politician and asked him to if he would be prepared to enter this house for the photographs and he agreed. My editor paid two thousand pounds for one picture to support our allegations and I opened an account for Raf. I arranged to meet with him last time I was here and that is why he was sitting on the wall, waiting for me. He now has his own bank account and money he can draw but not until the cheque has been cleared."

"I told him not to tell his father, and to use it for himself. I have no idea whether he listened to me, and the fact that he has now disappeared is rather worrying."

"I think the boy trusts me, and I have thought hard about finding ways for him to earn more money – legitimate ways, but of course, what he needs is a normal life and the chance to attend a decent school. He isn't simply another boy like any other boy. Bringing them into the UK was a spur of the moment decision. Raf's father did promise me background stories about the struggle in Palestine in return for bringing them in."

"I knew he was a conman but he was personable and resigned that most of his tricks were obvious and that people seemed to find him amusing rather than dangerous. Raf on the other hand hardly ever speaks. I suspect he may be thoroughly confused and brainwashed by his father and does exactly what he is told. But he strikes me as being an intelligent boy. Life in Palestine is weird, unimaginable, and the values more so."

The two men silently sip their coffee. Ralph is aware that Jon looks closely at him.

"Why the interest in Paul?" Jon asks softly.

"Have you ever read the Bible?" Ralph asks.

"I tried while at university, but I preferred the real world. The Bible to me is an extraordinary book of fiction written and edited by a lot of people with unrealistic perceptions and expectations. I do know that Paul lived in weird times when there were many religious merchants looking for customers to pay them money to perform physical or mental miracles. Whoever could claim the biggest miracle had the largest following. Even in those days Eastern techniques aimed at achieving a spiritual state attracted a lot of interest: now everyone takes dope instead. All highly improbable events that are outdone a thousand times every time by the films we watch on our television screens. At least Paul did not charge anyone anything but he was thrown in prison a few times, and it isn't quite clear why."

"You don't sound as though you believe in the power of your own mind?"

"I know some very powerful minds who have come a cropper when the chips are down. You're talking about believing in invisible things."

"It must have been quite a challenge for you to attend the meeting the other night, and again today. As you don't appear to have any faith it must have been sheer desperation looking for your next story."

"Well I confess I was promised you don't use a lot of biblical rhetoric and that you sound very down to earth even though you do talk about invisible things. My friends believe you. I know them well and that was a recommendation that I was prepared to accept on this occasion. I suppose the faith bit comes into reckoning when those listening to you go away and try to persuade themselves to believe in what you tell them. As you're all on your own, with no institutional support or backup that's quite a task. It's almost as though the world, or a very small part of it, hasn't really moved on since the days of Paul. Is that why you think Muslims and Christians should worship together?"

"Maybe. Sophistication is a huge threat to what the message of the Cross and Paul's Damascus experience is all about, but a bit of sophistication at this stage in history could do a lot of good. There are fundamental flaws in the way both religions are taught. With Muslims you have a section based on very nasty foundations that is trying desperately to hijack the support of others coming from the same Islamic background. Both religions suffer from the same threat – liberalism – not to be confused with freedom. With Christianity there is a calamitous weakening of truth and the reality of what happened in history to shore up a sweeping desire for the right to do anything, and everything if you can get away with it. It's called 'finding your identity' by doing anything you fancy even from the age of five or six without the warning that much of that could prove very destructive to the developing years."

"And do you blame inaccuracies in the way the two religions are taught?" Jon asks.

Ralph is thoughtful: "A lot of what is written was edited by individuals who chose their words to justify their own belief on how events unfolded and how it supports the prophecies of those who lived a few hundred years earlier. It was a difficult time, the construction of a religion to bind large groups of people into nationhood, living peacefully together, and learning to build a good life together."

"Today much of that may not be necessary anymore. If you're interested in hearing more, come to the next meeting. Perhaps I'll tell you what I think you want to know."

Jon pauses before asking: "And has your own research discovered where the Christians as well as the Muslims have gone wrong?"

"That is much easier than it may seem if you look at what is happening today," Ralph replies, "People have their own perceptions, and yet many millions accept what they are told. Even Paul, with his Damascus Experience had to find different words for different nationalities to overcome traditional cultures and scepticism. From a factual viewpoint there should be no difficulty at all in unifying the two religions. There is a powerful source for good at work in the universe and it stems from the acknowledgement of a kind and generous universal God. Your instincts may lean towards such a faith even though you're not yet fully aware of it."

"I see it with my eyes, and I hear it all around me."

"But Christians and their equivalents in other religions are as vain, self-righteous and selfish as all the remainder of the people living in communities anywhere in the world. The art of the conman is everywhere in public speaking. Stick as close to the truth as you understand it."

Jon sounds unsure of himself: "And how does Paul fit into all this?"

"Paul was an original. He was living proof that God exists and that Jesus is still alive. That is why he is worth reading and talking about. He might even be able to help you, but you have to have a clear mind before you approach him. And as things are, you very definitely have a huge hurdle to clear before you'll be able to make sensible contributions, but don't worry, your secrets are safe with me providing you don't make even the smallest attempt to compromise the freedom I have living in this church."

Ralph pours more coffee.

"Will your problem be easier if you hear the boys father is still alive, or would you prefer it if he was one of the two men killed?"

Jon turns away with an involuntary step side-ways.

Ralph continues: "Rafael – I presume that is his full name – sat on that wall outside for several hours waiting for you. He certainly has got patience."

Ralph silently drinks his coffee. Jon looks nervously at his watch and rises. "It doesn't look as though he has got the message to meet me here."

"Not yet anyway," Ralph says, "I'll look out for him."

Jon sounds troubled: "That might mean that his father is still a free man and that the two of them are on the run."

"Do they know where you live?"

Jon shakes his head.

Ralph purses his lips. "Interesting. Suddenly this address takes on a slightly different identity. I don't take that lightly. I have tried to make sure that no one sees this address as a place for dropouts, weirdoes or casual thieves to take advantage of. Terrorists never qualified for consideration before today. You had better keep me informed until you know what has happened to them. And don't push me. I will have no conscience about calling in Scotland Yard."

He reaches for a writing pad, jots down a number and hands it to Jon: "One bit of trust deserves another. Very few people have this number. I can see you may need help. But don't make me regret that I gave it to you."

Jon walks to door and after opening it pauses: "You have said I can come and listen to you when the others come again?"

Ralph chuckles softly "Are you by any chance wondering if there is enough in the story of Paul and his relationship with the Cross, that might help this young Muslim? I would say that depends entirely how open-minded this 13 year old can be? His age is on his side but don't expect him to be able to tear himself away from the land of his birth – just like that? You'll be welcome."

Jon nods his thanks and closes the door behind him.

Chapter Three

A group of seven young theology students, five men and two women, wait as Ralph carries an extra chair into the entrance to the nave. Some are sipping coffee from mugs. As they take their seats he leans on the chair with his elbows and says, "This has been an eventful week, if you read the papers or listen to the news. Some of us don't do this, or rarely, and of course we cannot ignore events around us if we really want to be involved with our fellow men and women."

"Paul never writes about the things which now fill our news bulletins every day. Wars, terrorism, and ordinary violence on the streets of our cities and towns feel a million miles away from the things we discuss and the spiritual awareness we wish to ignite among the very people making the headlines. It's as though life is out of control, with God, the police and everyone else reduced to mere bystanders and victims. Our only reassurance is that it is merely the minority attempting to assert their wills on the majority."

"I remain an optimist because I know what we're trying to do is growing more and more important. There is enough good will and human kindness in the world and the UK to stem the tide. A lot depends on individuals like yourselves and the strength of the message you wish to take to your congregations."

"I believe what I have to tell you will make your task easier, smoother and much more convincing and will strengthen the bond you will have with your parishioners. I see you as the new breed of clergy hoping to change the sliding influence of the C of E on public life. It will also leave you with a much more peaceful mind should you approach a time when you're preparing yourself to advance to the next phase of your life."

"I met with another group recently and they were all manifestly unhappy with the direction of Christianity in this country and in particular the C of E, and the way the message from God is preached. They revealed a particular resentment towards the media image of their Faith and also to the approach of education and the direction or non-direction showed by the government."

"I hear of an opinion poll stating that the most professional atheists will now be found among politicians, lawyers, teachers and journalists. So we're faced with an enormous uphill battle. I simply do not have the patience to have to argue with intelligent, educated people. We live in a democracy and we all have a right to an opinion on every matter under the sun. So be it. But not in this church."

"Some young Christians are wondering whether the time has come to take the same aggressive retaliation that they claim is aimed at Christianity. It's as though there is a movement developing, against what they perceive to be the peddlers of hate and destruction, that use the media channels to get their pernicious messages across – all in the name of freedom."

"Paul was confronted by threats of this kind almost on every front when he set out to convert the Gentiles. These days as you are undoubtedly aware he is unpopular in the C of E. People claim he is far too strict and difficult to understand. What nonsense. In his time misguided followers of the Torah accused him of being much too liberal. They said he courted popularity by creating a much easier road to God."

"Yet his message was straightforward and honest. The Law (the Torah and its 613 laws and conditions) stated clearly that anyone who broke one of these laws, was cursed and condemned forever. There was no way to repair the damage they had done to their own souls. Yet we know that the message from God through Jesus, was that He was a forgiving and a loving God. But added to this comes the warning from Paul that forgiveness is ours through the grace of God- it cannot be earned by ambitious individuals or deliberate action. The world has reached such a sophisticated approach to religion, that it is now possible to say to unwarranted minority groups – stop wallowing in what you are, and start striving to discover the real truth about yourself."

"Paul confirmed that Jesus was the first of a new humanity with a new covenant with God, and that everyone could become part of it. To the Torah adherents it sounded as thought Paul had hijacked the Jewish

God, but that was simply not the case. Style and culture has to be modified when the people go off the rails and perhaps the time is approaching for a reassessment of the way Christianity is being preached to practising Christians in this country. You seven here today could take part in that and play a full role. You must make sure that the power of God as well as knowledge of his Grace is restored to the Christian faith."

"Jesus always spoke about the Kingdom of God, but he wasn't always referring to the end product. Most of the time he was talking about people doing, thinking and approaching life on this earth in a different way, and if they listened to him, they would be entering into God's Kingdom long before they were ready for their moment of truth when passing from this life to the next."

"Paul ran into huge trouble from his fellow Jews because he was delivering the message that no one had to be Jewish to have access to God. For someone who had been a 100 per cent Jew all his life, and a Pharisee to boot, this was quite a U-turn. It brought him into opposition to such practices as circumcision, and the eating laws, none of which are relevant today to people like us for whom it was never part of our upbringing and culture."

"Paul saw himself as the new messenger taking the salvation promise to all nations. He found such immense joy in the knowledge that God had taken it upon himself to personally introduce a resurrected Jesus to him, that he wanted to spend his entire life proclaiming the wonder of God's power, his affection for his creation and his desire to have everyone back with him when their time arrived."

"But he was also an intelligent man inspired by an abundance of enthusiasm, determination and will power, and he concentrated heavily on the message of God's love, his sympathy for the problems facing mortals, and the stability of his never changing nature. This caused him to delay talking about his Father's righteousness until he understood exactly what it was. All around him there were passionate arguments, some of which spilled over into violence as individuals and groups fought one another's will-power and resilience to win over the minds of those who looked for a religious way to live. Paul concentrated in proclaiming God's trusting and loving nature while easing them away from traditional prayers that promised riches beyond their dreams for the poor and oppressed. This was one of the main reasons why Paul rarely used the accepted historical gospels to spread the word of Jesus. He relied heavily on his own Damascus experience and a new covenant with God. His message was new, his prayers were new and the covenant with God was new."

"Paul was never less than frank with his answers to the questions of those who sought conversion. He never accepted payment for his services, proved he was a strong believer in manual work to earn his way, and on personal issues spoke freely of his celibate way of life, saying that his relationship with God was the dominating factor in his life, and the relationship that controlled all the others. Celibacy was as normal for him as it was for Jesus."

"And he might have been talking to a group of students like you when he told them that the answers to their deepest problems, difficulties, uncertainties, frustrations, and feelings of guilt, could be resolved by committing themselves to a life with God through Jesus, and then getting on with the rest of their lives. Not everyone is able to draw on such massive inner-strength as Paul to live a life like he did- not everyone learned to cope with such a mixture of peace and divine inner discontent."

"There is no doubt that the media will continue to produce material which many Christians find offensive, obstructive and destructive. We are now living in a multi-cultural society and there is a great need for honest God-fearing politicians, but we also have to accept there are large groups of people living among us who have no time for meetings like this. But that is their problem, not ours – God knows many who die will not inherit continuous life, I know it. Our biggest enemies are those who think they are too clever by half."

"In Paul's time there were many very confused and uprooted people looking for some sort of religion to bring them peace of mind. And there was a huge variety on offer. But it all cost money. Not all that different from what is on offer today."

"The one God of the Jews would have come top if opinion polls had existed. People from everywhere were attracted to living a life with laws and rules to tell them what to do. It provided them with a sense of belonging. Other religions were formed taking parts of the Jewish faith, which suited them. But as the underlying goodness of God's love began to pervade normal life, it encouraged a belief over a hundred years or more BC that the world was a terrible place."

"And this belief fostered a hope among the Jews that their God would bring an end to this world and establish a new one."

"By the time Jesus came on the scene this belief and hope for a New World was widely accepted and discussed. Writers indulged in the fantasy of it all, how it would transpire, and what the new world would be like. And as the suffering of the Jews under the yoke of the Roman Empire intensified, so the Jews started looking forward to this great occasion, and the arrival of a Christ-Messiah to lead the way."

"There can be no doubt a powerful belief originated from an early faith that God cared for his people. It would be a world with no more injustice, wars, anxieties or death. Everyone would be happy, and all those who had died but had lived a good life, would be resurrected physically to become part of this new world."

"The way people believed in those days that God featured personally in the welfare of a nation is different from how we see things today. But that doesn't mean that God flows with the culture as it changes, mostly for the worse. God's nature will never change. His creation of male and female humans remains unchanged – they are either male or female and they are born with their natures blessed by God."

"For those who progress to a divine manifestation and gain understanding of the simplistic nature of judgement day, there is no problem. Saul was born in the time when it was thought that God would create a new wonderful world. He believed in physical resurrection. Even after his experience on the road to Damascus Paul still spoke about a physical resurrection. What happened to him was so vivid it was more real than anything he had ever seen in his life before. He just took for granted that he was introduced to the physical Jesus."

"He wasn't the only one who jumped to the wrong conclusion. Jesus appeared to Mary Magdalene and Cephas and a few others. When the disciples saw the empty tomb they took it for granted the physical Jesus had risen. There is no in-depth interview recorded with the chosen ones but there is absolutely no doubt that Jesus did appear to them individually. A collective manifestation would have been impossible.

That is not how God operates on the spiritual side of mortal life, and it simply underlines how much He values his relationship with each and every individual "

"The news spread about Paul's experience and his message of the one God and his crucified son who would return as a judge to put the world in order, bring justice to the poor and the oppressed and those without hope. It proved to be a gripping message and it gave Paul a tremendous lift and enhanced his commitment when he saw how his sermons took hold of congregations and turned them into individuals with a new perspective and massive hope for the future. Gone were the demons of depression and oppression as they became exuberantly and truly free."

"But it wasn't just the poor that benefited. There were many wealthy citizens who put their possession at the disposal of Christian communities – sponsors we would call them today – and Paul always praised them for their important contributions to his cause."

"While he insisted on doing manual work for his existence wherever he went, he accepted the offering of houses with rooms large enough for gatherings. And later when he spent a lengthy period in prison he was grateful for the gifts from his friends in Philippi."

"He strongly believed in having gatherings, groups, in order to spread his message and also to advance a refined, religious society preferring closer links with a life in the Spirit. Paul the visionary, looked ahead, and he saw the need to edify and sanctify the lives of those around him. He also knew communities would add strength to his message in his absence and that it would be important for believers to meet regularly to keep one another reminded of God's will in Jesus."

"We know a lot about Paul but even so, there is a lot about him which has not been properly documented. Articles written by him or about him were regularly rewritten during those times, because there was no media. It was done by those who wanted to keep their own record, as well as those who were in the same business as Paul and they used his messages, experiences and sermons to rewrite what they had written to justify their own claims, expectations and beliefs."

"It is suspected that some of his letters might have been slightly altered, as individuals either added to what Paul saw as his life's work or subtracted to suit their needs."

"Paul's opinion of himself, pre his Damascus Experience is well known. It wasn't good. He called himself a monster."

"This honesty might well have contributed to the suspicion of some former friends and allies while other fanatical adherents to the 613 laws of the Torah surely took exception to his sudden criticism that too many worshipped a book instead of a real God, whose love and compassion and understanding formed the basis of his relationships with humans. Jesus was the first to tell us about this wonderful new way to live and to endure the challenges facing us in our lives."

"Paul knew there were some people determined to kill him but fortunately his friends came to his rescue. The Damascus Experience remained his driving force. Whatever he said and whenever he said it, his joy knew no bounds at having been introduced to Jesus by the one living God."

"Paul believed everyone had the right to know the truth. He also knew there was a reason why God would not manifest in the lives of everyone. He understood that by giving a free will to every born baby God sacrificed his own ability to physically interfere with private lives. Unless there was an urgent need and it was deemed to fit in with His ultimate plan. Such occurrences are very rare."

"We know Paul had huge problems converting his own kith and kin in Jerusalem but there were already bunches of Christians who had either heard Jesus speak or had information handed down to them. To suddenly find in their midst a man who was known as a persecutor of Christians, to suddenly claim he was now wanting to do the exact opposite, to the detriment of his own lifelong and very firmly held beliefs, was difficult if not impossible to accept."

"Paul understood that and that helped to convince him he should concentrate on the Gentiles."

"He felt so strongly about this, and such was the strength of his personality and character and the influence of his Damascus Experience he was prepared to travel, by foot or any other way, to foreign lands to spread the word of his gift from the one and only living God."

"He was aware of other prophets and soothsayers who made all sorts of statements and claims of miracles but no one had the depth of understanding and insight that he possessed and his was the message that prevailed. And added to this, his message was free and his services were free whereas all the others made a living from what they had to say or do."

"There were other stories of blinding lights but it is not surprising that editors of the Bible stuck to the Damascus Experience. Even so, it is a mystery why they stuck to such an unworthy description of what had happened."

"Nothing deterred Paul because he knew his message carried with it the power, the glory and the only information about the next life and how to inherit this."

"There are a number of references to it, but it is only in reading everything several times, that one detects a line here and a line there that accurately reflects what had happened to Paul. Perhaps writers and editors felt it was so personal that it would be in danger of losing its value and power if described in full detail. That is a very valid point because there are no words to adequately describe in modern day terms the extraordinary majesty of such an experience."

"God does not manifest in any shape or form to individuals with closed minds. That simply will not happen. There are many different kinds of closed minds as well as open minds. There are 'open minds close to God' but only the few seem to obtain this status. Some modern day Christians appear to pay lip service to a chosen life style and to us they can be compared to Torah worshippers who believe without emotion, without trust, and without love."

"Saul started his journey to Damascus with hostility in his heart. He had every intention of finding a new group of Christians and persecuting them. We don't know exactly why or how fiercely personal Saul felt this hostility. We can suspect it may not have been as fierce as when he first started looking for Christians in order to demolish them with argument, or to have them imprisoned. Was he aware of the content of what Jesus told his listeners? Was there a slowly forming doubt urging him to find out more for himself?"

"But the fact that he felt compelled to embark on the journey was inspired by the innate determination which later gave him strength to promote the very cause he was now planning to destroy."

"There is no evidence that he had ever met or heard Jesus preach. His most obvious source of information must have been fellow Pharisees who had heard about Jesus and his preaching against the inhumanity of the Torah laws."

"We do not know at this stage whether it was the man Jesus or his message or both which seemed to disturb the worst elements of Saul's mind and psyche at that time in his life. Neither do we know whether he had read some of the sermons delivered by Jesus. If he had this might have challenged his adamant commitment to his Pharisee cause. Jesus spoke about a loving God, a forgiving God and he took issue against the heartless inhumane laws of the Torah. If at any time Saul had talked to people who had listened in person to the sermons he would surely have felt threatened by the support turning the Galilean into a cult figure, a possible King of the Jews, the Son of God."

"Having the sort of qualities and inner strength we later discovered he had, he might have wanted to know more for himself. The charge that the God of Jesus had a different nature to the nature of the Torah Laws might have sounded like a wake-up call. Be that as it may, Saul decided to go to Damascus to seek out those who were claiming to be followers of a man that had been crucified."

"On this occasion, to argue against them. No one knows what exactly was on his mind, but we do know God must have been watching, and He knew there was a slight opening taking place in the closed mind of Paul."

"It was a long journey but it gave him time to prepare himself. He was known in that part of the world as being a wordsmith and one who could become a persecutor of those whom he saw as a threat to the laws of the Torah."

"There are gaps in the records of Paul's life. As a Pharisee he would have been married because that is what was expected. There is no mention of what happened to his wife, or whether she had borne him a child. We suspect this part of his life caused him some unhappiness but he coped by stating simply that for him a celibate way of life was natural.

In his total devotion to a life with God it is perfectly natural he would never have given a thought to any other life style."

"The time came when he decided to have a rest and he may have seated himself on a rock to take a drink of water and perhaps some food."

"Was he mulling over his life, what he knew about Jesus and his sermons, looking for proof that he had no case to answer on behalf of the Torah? No man can seriously contemplate the sermons of Jesus without comparing them to his own set of rules and laws about life without concluding that his own life style was very shallow and light by comparison."

"The journey provided Saul with satisfaction because he was doing what he wanted to do, had done for most of his life, believed in, and he was confident he would be able to trace the new grouping because they appeared to have become known to those with a religious interest. He had confidence in his own ability to go into the basics of any argument and he had acquired the ability to demolish opposing arguments. He enjoyed asking himself testing questions and then having the answers in readiness."

"From everything that has been written about divine manifestations to mortals we know God cannot and will not make contact if there is no invitation. It always happens when least expected. It cannot be earned, pursued or manipulated."

"Prayer by devout people can create an elevated state of mind and peace but that is nowhere near to what was about to happen to Paul."

"There is no mention of time while Saul awaited what would prove to be the most defining moment in the history of the world."

"And when his eyes first became aware of it, it was nothing more than the slightest flicker of the tiniest light. It happened so quickly it very nearly didn't register in his mind. But it did, and it made him wonder if it was a mirage. But it did not interfere with his thoughts. He was enjoying playing Devil's Advocate with himself. And then he saw it again – a little brighter and was it slightly closer – the reflection of the sun on the wings of a bird? At the same time he felt a compelling need to return to the urgency and momentum of his arguments with himself. And then the light had disappeared again. He knew it could not have been a star because it was daytime – probably just the sun playing tricks on his eyes."

"Then suddenly he became aware of a presence hovering over his head, but he remained quite still as he pricked his ears and momentarily held his breath. When he had sat down he wasn't aware of any of the other travellers being close to him. The presence grew stronger and it forced him to move his head to both sides to see if there was anyone close to him?"

"There was no one. The air remained still, not a sound anywhere, and the nearest fellow traveller was in front of him. He too was resting."

"Was he trying to think too hard about too many different challenges? He wasn't! Damascus was the focus and the group of Christians he wanted to talk to was the target."

"He felt confident he could convince them of the strength of his own arguments. He started feeling felt a strange exhilaration in anticipation of reaching Damascus."

"Then he saw it again and it was in the same place, perhaps a bit closer, but still a distant flicker in a clear sky. He felt fascinated. It seemed to be static but then it slowly moved towards him. Or did he imagine it?"

"And then it was gone again but his eyes remained fixed on the same spot where it had been. He was determined to see it immediately should it return."

"As he waited his thoughts returned to Damascus, and looking for the group. Then the presence was back, feeling much larger and more powerful. This time he could not resist getting to his feet and making absolutely certain there was positively no one there. Feeling a bit bemused he sat down slowly. There was indeed no one anywhere near him. The sky looked even clearer than before and he wasn't sure whether he was focusing on the exact spot where it had appeared previously. He began to be concerned that if he blinked he would miss it and he felt himself stretching his eyes wider. He wanted to see. He felt so intrigued he knew he did not want the little light to disappear forever. Even Damascus and arguing with the Christians started losing its appeal."

"He wanted the light to remain, and he wanted it to come closer. His eyes could find nothing anywhere straight ahead, but then he sensed that the presence was slowly returning. This time he would not chase it away by getting up. And then the light was back – larger, and brighter. And now he was sure it was advancing towards him. He had no idea what it was but he knew he wanted it to come closer. He hardly breathed as he watched and waited."

"And still the light came closer, and the presence became massive but he felt totally unafraid and he resisted turning his head to check."

"He could feel the magnetic power of the huge light but it wasn't drawing him to it, it was the other way around. By now it was enormous, very bright but also completely unthreatening and he heard himself saying out loudly: 'I don't believe this, what is happening?'"

"And just as suddenly the light stopped. The power hovering around him withdrew slightly. He stopped breathing and then the light slowly started drawing back and moving away and to his dismay he felt the magnetic power pulling away. His arms and legs felt limp and as this feeling spread into his body he suddenly realised life was being drawn from his body by the retreating light."

"His cry was immediate and rang with fear: 'Don't go. I believe. I believe. I believe.'"

"And the light stopped and the presence stopped reducing in size and power and then the light came closer and grew gently into a massive presence and it slowly entered his body through his eyes and engulfed his body and mind and such was the ecstasy and glory that flushed through him he realised immediately he was in paradise in the presence of God."

"And just as suddenly a bearded man appeared in front of him and he saw the same light filling his body and he knew it was Jesus. And Jesus was alive. Then a voice resonated through him and he knew it was not the voice of Jesus. It said: 'Saul why are you persecuting me?'"

Ralph takes a deep breath before continuing: "He remained in this state of Grace for many hours and when it eventually eased away very gently Paul sank exhausted to the ground. He saw that most of the other travellers had gone ahead, but the one sitting ahead of him was still there. Paul staggered to his feet, dazed, disorientated, bemused, and stumbling like a blind man in need of help and guidance, and his fellow traveller came to his assistance."

"Try to imagine the man he had suddenly turned into, try to compare him to the man he was a few hours before. Saul who had been the monster had died and Paul, the international Gentile was in his place and in possession of the greatest secret ever revealed by God to a mortal. He was able to declare that God, the living, loving and forgiving God was close to the world and Jesus is alive and well. And he was able testify to that."

Ralph draws a deep breath.

"I want you to think about what I have said and then perhaps your questions will be more relevant."

One of the students raises an arm. "How does this experience of Paul compare with the manifestations of Jesus to Cephas and the disciples after the tomb had been found empty?"

Ralph takes a few moments before replying: "I think I can best distinguish between the two by saying Jesus simply appeared to Cephas and Mary Magdalene. It was like hearing a knock on the door and opening it, and there you are – Jesus in person. Except that there was no door and no knock. It just happened. It was in fact a perfect example of the symmetry between the spiritual and physical lives of those involved. It was not a physical appearance by Jesus and the occasion may have lacked the majesty of what had happened to Saul but it lacked nothing of the power or reality. When it is said in the Bible that Paul had other divine revelations that is what had happened to him. There were no further messages and this was probably because these occurrences, in their rarity, simply provided the recipients with re-assuring reminders of the world to come. They never last long but they are as real as anything that the eyes can behold. It would be incorrect to say that manifestations of this kind happen without the presence of God, when in fact they could not happen without his power."

"There are characters in the Old Testament who may have been blessed in this manner. Another explanation could be that these manifestations personified an intimacy with the Holy Spirit that comes as a reward for achieving a highly elevated state of mind, close to God, without knowing how it was done, and without having the expectation of a reward. When Jesus made his appearances they came as a consolation for grieving friends, who must have felt intolerable isolation and threat following his horrendous death."

CHAPTER FOUR

Ralph finishes a punishing short spell on the treadmill and reaches for a towel as he steps off. A sudden irresistible urge to look through the front door spy-hole reroutes him from walking towards the shower room.

He had had a call from Jon Singer shortly after breakfast saying he had not yet heard from Raf. The police still hadn't identified the dead suspected terrorists, but one was said to be a 16-year- old teenager. He sounded concerned and stumbled for an answer to Ralph's question as to whether it was time to discuss his difficulties with the police.

His expectation of not seeing anyone outside causes him to have to take a second glance before he spots the young boy, wearing the same clothes as the last time, sitting in almost exactly the same place on the wall. He feels so taken aback that he immediately draws away as though afraid he might have been seen.

Without another moment's hesitation he walks swiftly towards the rear and a landline telephone near the door leading to the kitchen. After dialling and recognising Jon's voice, he says, "The boy is here, sitting almost in exactly the same spot on the wall where he was the last time while waiting for you. It's as though he has never left the spot and I have no idea how long he's been there. This was the first time since before your earlier call that I remembered to check, and there he is."

Silence, then Jon mutters. "I'm in the middle of some work. Would you mind inviting him inside and telling him I'll be there as soon as I can make it. I'm only minutes away depending on the traffic. Perhaps you can get him to talk without asking the sort of questions that might cause him to clam up. I doubt if he knows about events in North London or what might have happened to his father. Please don't let him go away. He hasn't answered my calls and that can only mean something might be wrong with the mobile. If that is the case he won't know anything about the shoot-out at the safe house. I've never had problems getting him to talk to me, although he's a listener rather than a talker. Whether he'll be different now that he's faced with the prospect of being without his father remains to be seen. I'm not trying to put words into your mouth. Handle it anyway you see fit but please don't let him get away."

He barely breathes as he rattles away, "The details of what happened in North London remain obscure, not just to me, but also, I suspect to the police. I have no idea what his father was doing in north London. For that reason I don't know what the immediate future holds for the boy and whether he was aware this sort of emergency might arise and what his options are if any. On the journey from Paris to London most of the talk was about life in the UK and the prospects of the father finding work. There was no mention of friends until we reached London. I accept he is my responsibility but I'm not sure I know what that means."

"He has no other relatives that I am aware of – his mother died during an Israeli bombing raid. I do apologise for drawing you in to this and I do appreciate I am prevailing on the sort of person you are. Please don't take any decisions or action until I have had a chance to talk to the boy. I am responsible for his presence in this country, and I am prepared to take the risk of driving him back to France or where ever he wants to go. I know it sounds as though I am trusting you to do the right thing, and I admit I am taking advantage, but this is why I came to see you in the first instance."

"Perhaps Raf will tell you what he thinks and feels about Christianity. He's a Muslim, but I have no idea what that means. I became attracted to his plight in Gaza City and at first I thought he wanted to come to the UK for a new life. Then his father appeared on the scene and I felt compelled to bring both."

"Get here as soon as you can," Ralph says and returns to open the front door with a towel around his neck. The boy looks up, jumps from the wall and waits.

Ralph walks up to him: "So we meet again Raf. My name is Ralph. It's like your name but I have an L to make sure it is pronounced slightly differently. I've just spoken to Jon and he has asked me to invite you inside and for you to wait for him. Do you understand what I'm saying? He'll be here as soon as he can. Are you happy with that?"

The boy nods and they walk silently towards the front door. Ralph shuts it after letting the boy enter first. Then he almost walks into him as Raf stops and looks intently around the almost empty nave.

"What sort of church is this?"

"It is my own private church."

"Are you your own private priest?"

"Yes you could say that."

He walks slowly into the centre and continues to look at the walls, and then focuses his attention on the gym for a few moments.

"Do you play a sport?"

"Exercise is good for me and I enjoy doing it."

"Are you Jon's Imam? Does he come here to see you about his problems?"

"He has recently attended when I have held group meetings."

"Am I his problem?"

"You've been missing. Jon has tried to telephone you. He was very worried. London is a very big city."

"I've been waiting for my father. He went to visit friends and now he is lost I think. London is a big city."

"Jon mentioned your father."

"Did they speak?" This time there is an urgent tone in his voice.

"No they have not spoken, and that worries him as well. Do you know where your father might be?"

"He went to see friends – a long way with the Tube. I went there once but I could not find it again."

"Were they business friends of your father?"

Raf continues to look around the church.

"Yes, from Palestine. They came to this country a long time ago. There are others as well."

"From other countries?"

"I think so. They have business to talk about with my father."

"Are you planning to live in England?"

There is a long pause before he replies: "I do what my father tells me to do."

"What sort of work does your father do?"

"We work for Allah – he is our god."

"Did they have this meeting in a temple for Muslims?"

Softly, looking straight ahead of him. "He said there was a temple but he did not say if he was going to go there. He went to a house. Are you a Christian?"

"Yes………" There is a long pause and the boy turns expectantly to face him.

"Do you know anything about the Christians?" Ralph asks.

"You support the Jews and we don't like your laws. Your god is not the same as ours. There are many differences."

"The differences are not as big as you think."

"We don't like your laws because it only helps the Jews. You give them money and you give them weapons to kill us."

"Why are you here in this country?"

"I came with my father who has business to do and he needs my help. What sort of Christian are you? My father says there are many different churches. For us a Muslim is a Muslim. I have my Imam and if I have a problem he helps me. I trust him. Does Jon trust you?"

"At this moment I think he does. Do you like Jon?"

"He is my friend. Without him we could not have come to this country."

"You have done some work for him?"

"He told you that? Then he must trust you." His curiosity gets the better of him.

"Do you train every day? My Imam could never even walk fast? He would die immediately." There is no humour in the tone of his voice. Ralph looks curiously at him. "Do you like sport?"

"We do not have things like this where I live. I can kick a ball, but anybody can do that."

He gets up and walks to the punch bag and gently hits against it and then inspects his hand. Ralph arrives at his side.

"You must not hit the bag without gloves and you must make a proper firm fist like this and connect with this part of the fist or you will hurt your hand, perhaps even break a bone."

Raf carefully makes his fist as was explained to him and then hits the bag. He nods in approval. Ralph steps away and says: "I am going to have a shower. Jon will be here soon. Can you look after yourself while I wash? If you want to work out in the gym go ahead, and afterwards you can have a shower."

Raf walks towards a large old painting hanging on the wall and studies it closely.

"We don't hang pictures like this in our temples."

"This is a very private place," Ralph says softly. "I don't have any religious rules in here. The people who come here have a reason for wanting to do so. Occasionally a stranger knocks on the door and asks to come inside just to rest and think. They come here because we worship one God, a very caring, and forgiving God who promises continuous life for those who love him."

The boy looks uncertain as he says softly: "My Imam says Christians are mad. They have many enemies and they don't resist in any way. If you believe in something why don't you fight to protect it? My Imam says democracy is weak and full of holes for their enemies to use against them. Do you lock your doors?"

"Not all the time. We rely on freedom to protect our way of life. If everyone has the same freedom under the laws of this country, we trust they will obey the laws to protect our way of life. That is our strength. But of course not all people enjoy obeying the laws of government. Under this system we can choose how we want to worship God."

"Are there many bad people in London?"

"Have you had problems since you've been here?"

He shakes his head. Ralph continues: "I prefer individuals to make arrangements to see me, or to visit this Church. I would not like it if a gang of hooligans came here to challenge me. Or a gang of religious fanatics so I do not offer the usual kind of services that normal churches do. As long as I know who they are they are welcome but I don't turn all strangers away."

"How much do they pay to come to you for advice?"

"It is free. No one pays anything to come here. I don't see myself as a teacher. I offer information to people who want to listen. I do not encourage arguments nor am I particularly interested in other religions. What I say is not for discussion. Some of the things I tell people will be new to them. I also know which things will puzzle or even confuse some and I make a point of explaining properly, so that there is no need for questions. That is my only rule. I am content with what I have to say. I offer the truth, as it exists for me. Those who come to listen have the choice to take it or leave it. There are many things in the Christian religion that need to be put right, just as there are things in the Muslim religion that need to be put right."

"Are you trying to do that? What sort of things do you think are wrong?"

Ralph is aware of the interest showing in the eyes of the boy, before he replies: "I speak my mind most of the time because I believe the time has come to correct some of the misapprehensions in the Christian faith. The time is right to make people aware of the changes that must be made. There is nothing different about the fundamental truths that I share with other Christians it is simply that I have discovered forgotten details. Worshippers are being turned away because leaders have lost track of the nature of the God they profess to worship. They are imposing their own nature on their god, and I'm sure you will agree they are seriously travelling in the wrong direction. Sometimes the changes are tenuous and fragile, but immensely important because they point in a different direction. I have only been living here for a short time. I do not yet know how things will develop. It is all a huge experiment. I'm very glad you're here because I suspect you take your religion very seriously don't you?"

Raf looks silently into his eyes as he nods his head in agreement. Ralph continues: "I hope you and I can talk about it?"

"But you said you are not interested in other religions?"

Cautiously: "What I have to say does not really have anything to do with institutional religion. It's more about relationships and a way of life and doing things. Paul had this problem. He grew up to be a certain person and worshipping God in a different way. His parents were involved with the Torah way of life and Saul followed them. He saw it all differently, as though his mind was at least half shut to the realities that were waiting for him to discover."

"He wanted others to accept this way of life. God thought otherwise and he saw in Paul someone who could promote the message of Jesus and the truth about his crucifixion. So when Paul travelled to Damascus where he intended to persecute Christians God drew Paul into his presence in the most wonderfully amazing way."

"Just like Gabriel did to Mohammed!"

Ralph is thoughtful and says slowly: "Well now brace yourself, Raf. You're forcing me to say something, which you may not like but I am not being critical of you personally. No one else has the power of God the Creator. Only He has the power to draw living people into what we call an elevated consciousness of the next life. He would not have called himself Gabriel if he had decided to reveal his power to Mohammed. There is absolutely no way Mohammed might have misunderstood a revelation involving God. His presence cannot be confused with someone or something else. I know Jesus is with God and also Paul. I have seen them talking to one another. But they do not share power with their Father."

Their eyes meet. The boy waits expectantly and Ralph continues: "God is great and God is good, I have heard Muslims say on television and in newspapers. I agree with that. But he is more than that. God created the earth and heaven and us. He is indeed very powerful but he is also caring, and protective and forgiving. He does not need anyone or anybody to help him do what he believes he must do. He does not have a right hand man or a left hand woman. God does it himself. When somebody dies God is there. If many die together he is there for everyone. God controls life and death because that is what the world is all about. We don't know what other plans God has for the life he created on earth, but we do know he has plans, because he goes to a lot of trouble to protect and personally receive every person who is moving from this life to the next. There is no way anyone can deceive God. That is the extent of his power."

"Your Mohammed was a clever and powerful leader. He lived 600 years after Jesus and he used many of the good things that Jesus said and also took from the history of the Jews. There is nothing wrong with that.

He did the right thing, but perhaps he did not go far enough. This could easily be put right."

Raf listens intently and then asks: "Are you saying Mohammed met God the way Paul did?"

"No, I am not saying that Raf, that is the bit that I'm not sure about. If Mohammed claims he had had a divine revelation then I cannot refute that. But I if he had had a meeting of the sort that Paul had had he would not have wanted to say it was with Gabriel. He would not have been in any doubt. God does not play games with the way he appears to people on this earth."

"There is no way God would have made a mistake. So why did Mohammed call his manifestation a meeting with Gabriel? Perhaps you'll be able to help me figure that one out? It is worth thinking about, but not worth worrying about. I think you're an intelligent boy who likes to think about all the different things that happen in life. If everybody was like that there would be far fewer problems in the world today."

The boy sounds cautious: "And what about the Christians? You say they also have got things wrong? Is it to do with Jesus becoming alive when he was dead?"

"That's it exactly Raf. It did happen but not in the way many leaders are saying it happened. Our preachers do not have the same authority as your Imam. Some people who go to church don't believe a word the preacher tells them. Their democratic rights warn them to be sceptical. And the Bible says some very strange things that are difficult to understand."

"Jesus was seen by several people after he was crucified and that is exactly what happened. But whoever edited the Bible did not really understand how and why these appearances to a very few people were possible, and those who did not have such an experience doubted that the others had had it. Jesus did not appear to a group of people at the same time. That is not how it happened. He appeared to one at a time. It was a terrible time and the followers of Jesus must have felt threatened. Some must have feared for their own future. God wanted people to appreciate that going to Heaven, or Paradise as you prefer, is very straightforward and available for all the people living on earth."

"This is not how Christianity is preached in many churches today. Resurrection means switching from physical life to spiritual life and it starts taking effect immediately. Otherwise the soul is lost. When you leave this earth you make contact with the presence of God and that draws you into life with Him if that is your destiny. No one knows exactly how long that takes – minutes, maybe quicker? You don't have time to argue, of that you can be sure. I think when you make contact – the real you, which is your true nature, the way you were born and the way you lived your life, knows very quickly if you're going to make it into the presence of God. Only God has the power to control and smoothen this transference from physical to spiritual life. It is each individual's once in a lifetime time opportunity. There is no second chance. When Jesus appeared to the people after he had been crucified, he was already with God. Appearing to the chosen few could only have happened through the grace of God."

"It is a moment, or moments, when miraculously the recipient is blessed with a completely open mind to receive such an event. It is very rare. It is wonderfully quiet and a totally unexpected occurrence. It is so vividly special that some people to whom it has happened prefer to keep it to themselves. But perhaps that can be seen as being selfish. God doesn't like selfish people."

"When Paul was introduced to Jesus on the road to Damascus something very special happened to him and he never forgot the details. It gave him the gift of drawing so much closer to God when he needed to be, and that gave him the insight that no one else was blessed with at that time."

"You can forget everything I have said to you but remember that life does not end for those people who love God, and who have lived their lives to be with him. That does not mean you can't have normal lives, working, getting married, having children and having ambition to help others live the same sort of life. Paul knew just what an unbelievable place heaven is and he wanted everyone to know about it, especially non-Jews – the Gentiles. People like you and me."

Raf whispers: "My mother loved and trusted God. She said for people like us that is the only way to live and to have any chance to become rich. She knew some have to make sacrifices, and fortunately Allah approved of what we should do. But she did not like the war."

Ralph sighs deeply: "Well Raf if you learn to really love God, then you are in for a number of very pleasant surprises. If you believe God is a good and a forgiving God and that you must treat other people, as you want others to treat you, then one day you will find your mother again. You may have to change some of your expectations. For Christians there are no big houses or motorcars in heaven, but there are riches beyond your dreams. Life will be much more exciting and of course, you'll see your mother again."

Raf, as though remembering a crucial point: "What about bodies? The people who saw Jesus, what did they see?"

Ralph's response is immediate: "They saw Jesus looking more real than anything they had ever seen in their lives before, and that was because the power of God's presence was helping them."

Thoughtfully: "My mother said there are many bad spirits in Palestine? Where do they come from?"

"The more I hear about your mother the more I like her. We have demons in this country as well, but because of our traditions we have learned to rub along with them. Another time I will tell you about the Spirit of Paul and how he battled against demons in people, and people who acted like devils to prevent him from interfering with their own brand of culture. You must learn to love God in return or your chances of inheriting eternal life will not be very good. You can't just say "OK I'm a Christian" and then carry on like a hypocrite, or a crook, or a barbarian or a politician. How you live your life is vital because it affects your mind."

"Now! I need a shower. There is a tin of biscuits on the kitchen table. You must be hungry. Help yourself. It's for my guests, and that includes you."

When Ralph returns 20 minutes later he finds Raf sitting at the kitchen table eating from the almost empty biscuit tin. "I thought you might be hungry. Jon will probably take care of that for you, otherwise you can help me prepare a meal in a while. Did you know that the food you eat is also good for your mind?" He smiles.

"Yes I know. When I am hungry for a long time I can't think. The Imam warned me not to listen to Christians. But you say you are not really a Christian."

"Oh but I am. I love a God that does not like it when people go to war. He wants children to grow into adults, and to marry and have children, but he knows that every person has their own strong will and that we are living in times when every person tries to be themselves rather than be part of a Christian community where everyone lives in peace with one another. So he has a problem. There are too many bad laws in too many countries, and people are beginning to rebel against this. People want to be free and they have a great need to be free. That is what Jesus taught us. We need to be free so that we can learn to rely on the grace of God, and his forgiving nature, to inherit continuous life."

Raf is thoughtful then he says cautiously. "I think my mother would have liked you. I feel close to her because I feel I might soon be joining her. In Palestine we cannot see how life will be normal. The Jews are powerful because they are supported by the British and the Americans. Allah understands this. Does your God understand it too? I would like to have what you call continuous life."

"God is not interested in politics Raf. Jesus was against the inhumanity of man against man. He wanted everyone to be free to worship the one and only God. Those who love God have no problems with life, and with the people around them. They are friends with everyone. You also believe in one very powerful God. You have said so. It isn't easy to change the way you believe, even if you continue to believe in the same God. We are all made in His image. So if you are prepared to look at life differently, and pray for God to help you, you will discover what His true nature is, and it's no big deal. You can trust God, but the trust must be for inherited continuous life in his presence. The moment you start asking for a football, or bicycle or a palace, you know he can't hear you. We don't know or understand how and why God seems to ignore so many bad things in this life and so we have to learn to look after ourselves, and our family, and our friends, and their friends. That is a very good beginning, and if every day we ask Him to help you, there will be days when it will seem as though God is walking hand in hand with you as you cross the many very busy roads in life."

He takes a breath and looks closely at the boy, who in return looks straight at him, waiting for him to continue. He does. "So you have problems and I have problems, and your god Allah has the same problems as my God. Both suffer from the fact that too many people do not understand what the true nature of God is. And as I have said, the choice is yours. Paul tells us all the nations of the world must become God's people and if we accept that God loves us, wants us back when we leave this earth then we will learn in turn to love him. He is just as interested in you and me and your father as anyone else." He pauses, "Do you have any idea where your father might be?"

Ralph holds his breath as he waits for the answer. The boys voice sounds flat and matter of fact. "He will join us when he is ready. And I have to make sure I will be ready. I ask my mother to help me but I'm not sure she hears me. My father has been very busy. Life in Palestine is difficult. He will deserve to be rich. He needs money very badly and that is why we are here. Perhaps some time you can talk to him but that won't be easy, my father thinks he knows everything. Can I walk around your church just to look?"

"Of course."

"You can walk with me if you don't trust me. Tell me more about your kind of Christianity and why are you here on your own? Why do you offer people free advice? How will you live? Why did God need Paul to help Jesus if he is so powerful? If he wants everybody back why does he make it so difficult?"

"I have often wondered about it as well Raf. The biggest mystery of all is that God gave every person a free will to do exactly what they like and how they want to do it. That must be tied up to the future plans of God. By giving you a free will, and a very powerful will at that, he knows he will not make it easy for you to learn to love a mysterious invisible God who created all men and women equal and then put them in different places on this earth and watched them develop."

"Most of what happens to you is influenced by yourself, the decisions you make, the bad judgements and the good ones, even in Palestine. He also gives you the ability to like other people and if you like others more than you like yourself then you are on the right road."

"We all have to learn to trust God, because in that way we learn to trust people and that will inspire you to help others."

"Things got so bad during the time of Jesus and Paul that for two hundred years before they were born almost everybody thought the earth was a terrible place. Life was so unpleasant and difficult that everyone with the ability to think, felt sure God would send a super-hero to come and change the world into a wonderful new place."

"He not only did that, he went much further, but it did not happen in the way people expected. He sent Jesus and then Paul to explain that there is no need to change the earth. If people train their powerful wills to think differently, to do things differently, and to live their lives differently they will get the biggest surprise they can possibly hope for when their time is up."

"So it is not too difficult to understand there has to be reason for making the business of living and dying complicated. God knew this was going to be difficult. That's why he gave us brains, some understanding if we try to figure it out for ourselves, courage and determination to commit ourselves to a wise and selective lifestyle, and the ability to run for our lives when we have to. We must not be reckless with our lives. There is a lot that we can do to contribute, even if only to our friends, and especially if we are part of a family with children growing up with care and love they become part of a wonderful tradition. This tradition is part of the Spirit of God and Jesus and Paul and Mohammed. There are so many things we can do for ourselves to enjoy this life before moving on to even greater fulfilment in the next life."

"How far away is your Heaven?"

"God is near. Every time someone dies he is there. He has to be. It is his law. Every person meets with him, even if only for a very short time, to see if they inherit the chance to be with him. Sometimes, very rarely, he reveals himself in a very personal and powerful way to an individual. It can happen to you, although I have to warn you such an event doesn't happen easily to someone your age unless you are a particularly gifted kind of person, with the ability to understand what it is that has happened to you. From what I can see of you, you are normal, healthy and intelligent. You are able to listen without wanting to argue and who knows, it may be your task one day to help those Muslims who have lost their way?"

Raf seems lost in thought as Ralph asks gently: "Are you interested in religion?"

"I miss my mother and I will do whatever I have to do to be with her."

"Are you planning to go back to Palestine?"

"My father will make the decision."

"So there is a possibility you might decide to live in England."

Raf frowns: "I do not know how to answer that. My father will make the decision. This Paul, is he rich and powerful, like Jesus?"

"Yes, he's probably one of the richest men there is and he is powerful because at this very moment he is close to God. He knows more than you and I put together."

The boy sounds pensive: "I don't know very much. I have to ask the Imam if I have a problem, but my friends and I don't ask him too often because we are worried what he will ask us to do. I don't see him often. Where I live everyday we have to be clever to stay alive. No one wants to die by an Israeli bomb or bullet. Before we came to London I asked the Imam what should I do and he said Allah wants me to come, and he said I must be brave because London is a bad city with many bad people who will try to make me think Allah is not the right god for me."

Ralph waits before saying thoughtfully: "In this country we believe we decide for ourselves what we want to believe. That is the democratic way to live. It might not be the right way but we are free to decide for ourselves. We are confident that is what God wants for everyone. That is why it is so very important to have the right leaders – people who know about the nature of God."

"In Palestine we believe Allah tells us what to do and for that we ask the Imam," Raf replies. "I must be told because my life is different from what I see when I walk through the streets here in London. I know Allah is powerful and great and he wants us to work for him, but I do not know what to do, so I listen to my father. If I do that Allah will let me live with my mother."

"Have you spoken to some of the people who live in London?"

"Only where my father and I stay with friends. When I travel I ask for help and everybody tells me what to do. But in the streets and the tube trains nobody talks to me. I can now travel without asking many people to show me where to go. I can read English and Allah is good to me. I have heard no bombs falling anywhere. But that is because the English are a powerful nation and they have very big bombs they can explode. We do not want to have a war with England but some of your politicians are very bad."

He is unsure of himself and looks expectantly at Ralph for his reaction..

"Well that is one of the weaknesses of a democracy, Raf. Sometimes politicians are so clever at being dishonest they manage to fool the people who vote to put them in power, most of the time, and then the others who did not vote for them have to accept this and live with it. It isn't easy but in order to have peace rather than people going around shooting one another we have learned to be patient and hope our own politicians can learn to lie as well as the others and take control. I say that deliberately because many people have stopped voting in protest against this fashion of politicians not telling the truth."

Raf gives him a curious glance, pauses, and then says, "In Palestine it is different. Sometimes we have to fight to get rid of people who are bad. Allah says so. Do you pray direct to your God?"

"Of course. For a long time many people have preferred to pray through a saint, but there is enough evidence now that God does not disapprove of direct contact."

"In Gaza some people pray for a very long time. Sometimes I say the same thing many times to make it longer. Do you think that is wrong? Maybe Allah did not hear me the first time so I ask him many times."

Ralph makes sure his tone is sympathetic, "Well, I have never tried to pray to your Allah so I can't advise you how to do it."

"Do you think Allah is very different from your God, the father of Jesus? How do we know God forgives our sins?"

Ralph sounds cautious: "Well that is what faith is all about. That is why Paul is such a good example. He admits he acted like a monster towards many people during the times when he persecuted Christians, but even so God drew him into his presence and introduced him to Jesus.

Surely he would not have done that if he had not forgiven Paul his sins? And we also know that Paul would not have been on the Damascus Road at that time if Jesus had not been crucified. Paul believed if Jesus had not died his sins would not have been forgiven."

The boy slowly nods his agreement then asks: " Do you teach people how to pray?"

"The best prayer always comes from the heart Raf," is his swift reply. "One of the best prayers I can think of is very simple and very short. If you are worried, troubled, afraid, fall to your knees and say: 'God please help me, help me, help me'. Then ask yourself what you need help for and if you know your request is selfish you must change your request because you won't receive the help you want. If you are in trouble and you can honestly pray for someone you know who is also in trouble, then you're travelling in the right direction."

Silence as Raf lowers his eyes to stare at the floor. Ralph says softly: "Does that remind you of your present situation? Perhaps now you understand my saying we are not all that different. I like the way your mind works. Long prayers are irrelevant. I try not to confront God with my domestic problems and I know he won't and can't change the world with a flash of lightning. It does not work like that. If you are troubled, worried or afraid, think about the power of a God who loves you, and who will forgive you your sins, providing you know what you have done wrong. And if you are travelling, driving a car, ask God to protect the other drivers who will be on the roads with you and try not to crash into them. When you start thinking like that you are knocking on the door of the Kingdom of God. That will teach you to drive carefully and that will also protect your own life."

Raf sounds curious. "Sometimes Christians go to church in a crowd. If your God appears to people one at a time what is the point of going in a crowd. Is it because they don't know or are afraid to meet with their God on their own?"

Ralph smiles, saying: "I'm sure you've just made God smile Raf. Going to Church is a celebration for Christians who believe deeply, or that is how it should be. Time off from working all week and struggling with the problems we all have in our lives. Paul said very often, for him death would be a gain, because he wanted to get back into the presence of God."

"Some of the meetings I have here are with students with enquiring minds."

"But you said you don't allow them to ask questions."

Ralph smiles again as he looks into the solemn eyes of the boy. "I have done a lot of research about Paul because I think the English Church is doing him a disservice. I have a few clergymen who send me people who want to listen to what I have to say. Some of this is new and different. At least, it isn't spoken of in public often, as far as I know. So who can argue against what is new? I like Paul because he was like us, and he lived in your part of the world. He started the Christian churches because he wanted everyone to know that God is completely unique and available to every person on this earth. He was the first alive person who was shown by God what it is like to be in His presence and he also showed him that Jesus, who was crucified, is still alive. That is very important news. Modern life can get so sophisticated we lose track of what the origins are and then we think the only way to improve things is to change the nature of God. I'm sure you agree that when you start tampering with the Truth you are heading for serious trouble."

"I like Paul. In modern terms he was a real hero in every way, because he found so much opposition from so many different kinds of people, and yet all he wanted to do was to tell people about continuous life. But he had problems. People were prepared to accept that he had had this wonderful divine experience on the road to Damascus, but when he tried to tell them how they should live their lives, he found that their culture, their habits and their will to control their own lives, did not want to co-operate. He was a man like us. His own people knew the sort of man he was before God appeared to him, and they did not trust him."

"There were many other fake prophets trying to make a reputation for themselves by claiming all sorts of things, and they weren't sure about Paul and his story that he had been in the presence of the one and all-powerful invisible God."

"The Jews were passionate people and they believed their bible, the Torah, with its 613 laws was how one should live. But the laws were for the Jews only and they said you had to become a Jew before you could be welcomed to their God. But then God explained to Paul that all people are welcome in Heaven and Paul decided to tell as many people as he could the great news. It is an amazing story because Paul, before his experience on the Damascus road, was a man who did not like Christians and he travelled about arguing with them and getting them thrown into prison. That was a time when people could not discuss religious problems without getting angry, and upset and feeling threatened. I hope you don't feel threatened now."

Raf is thoughtful but remains silent. As Ralph continues, "God works in mysterious ways sometimes and his decision to draw Paul into his presence is a good example, simply because it showed Paul what a forgiving God he is, and also it proved Jesus was not dead. It was a very important event and it is strange the way that writers in the bible should hold back from explaining what exactly had happened. There is so much confusion these days caused by the distorted things said about Christianity, sometimes even by ordained clergymen. They are all protected by the laws of democracy, when they should be sacked."

"Paul spent the rest of his life telling people about his experience. Everything he ever said was in praise of the generosity of God in choosing him to take the message to the Gentiles – a simple straightforward message – no one needs to die. Life is continuous for those who learn to love God, and they will only learn this if they will accept that in turn he is a loving and forgiving God. If you live the right sort of life and you learn to love your God, you will never die, but you do leave your body behind. You'll be amazed how many Christians are confused about this. Of course we must blame the leaders who are ignorant themselves and who set bad examples."

Raf is thoughtful. "But what is your reward in heaven? In Palestine we know we can die any time. So some choose when they want to die. They become martyrs and for that they are given riches in paradise. What does your God give you?"

Ralph takes his time before saying: "That is wrong Raf. Why should God want people to die before they have to, when he knows it is going to happen anyway? He gives people free wills to make everyone individual. That means he expects you to make a contribution to the life around you, even if you just work for your neighbour. If you die before your time is up then this might interfere with the God's plan for you. If you don't know what that contribution should be, the safest thing for you is to try and find out. You might be wrong a hundred times, and then you might say to yourself that you're trying to bribe God, but at least you will have made an effort. If you wish to die before your time, you are fighting against the will of God and that is a terrible decision to make. Today this is quite a problem because so many hospitals are keeping people alive when they would much rather move on. It is the fashion."

"We have never been told about the plans of God but we do know he wants every person back. That is the most important fact of every life, and we must never ignore it. If we knew everything that God has in mind for every person, life would be too easy and even boring and no one would want to do anything on earth anymore. As soon as a baby was old enough to think, it would kill itself because life with God was so much better. Your relationship with God is very personal, and earning the right to continuous life is very challenging. I can only tell you about some of the things that I have learned since studying the life of Paul but then it is up to you. I tell some people they will not go to heaven simply because they go to a church every Sunday. Too many Christians go because they try to make deals with God. It is very easy to understand if you don't love God how can you trust him, and this trust will build up through hope, faith and the belief that the road you have chosen to enter into God's Kingdom will have prepared you to be drawn into the presence of your Creator and continuous life. That is the only way you can be justified and fulfilled. That is why we have to listen to Jesus and Paul, even in this day and age. First we start by learning that God loves us and that he will forgive us many things. If this does not teach us to love in return then we know we have been trying to deceive ourselves, and even worse, deceive God. If you put your own interests before your relationship with God, then you are in very serious trouble."

A thought strikes Raf and he asks: "Is that why many people go together to church to help one another?"

Ralph is thoughtful. "Yes. It is a special kind of friendship. People go there not because they are looking for something, but because they want to spend time with their friends away from all their problems and challenges and simply thank God for being there, for giving them strength, for making them happy and content, and for giving them the minds to help other people enjoy life in the same way. Unfortunately these days very misguided politics interfere with the minds of too many priests. The same has happened in your country where some of the Imams have joined the fight and they ask their followers to go to war. In this country there are different wars. Too many people want to do what they like, when they like, and as often as they like, even if this destroys the values we know must exist for a normal happy family life which will lead us to a life with God afterwards."

"Too many people only believe in what they can see, eat, drink, and feel and they don't like thinking too much for themselves. It is too easy to ignore what someone else says, thinks or experiences. In schools there is now a strong emphasis to teach children from the age of four to be themselves whatever they might imagine they are. It is simply another way to encourage individuals to be totally inward looking and selfish. Misguided writers want to dictate what the culture of our time should be. They deceive themselves by saying Christianity says you can be redeemed in your dying moments just like the man who was crucified next to Jesus."

"Their minds have not been conditioned to love the invisible. Neither have they ever felt his power. For reasons we do not know, God only reveals bits of the next life to a few people – like Paul. With him God chose well because he was such an amazing man."

"Paul understood he had to continue with the new way of life that was started by Jesus and in doing so he decided to abandon the old ways of talking about and praying to God. He knew what the crucifixion of Jesus really meant, and he understood the truth of what Jesus had preached. He was himself a bad man before this happened and for the rest of his life he was always praising God for forgiving him and giving him another chance."

"He first thought the Christians were his enemies, but real Christians don't want to go to war. Sometimes they are forced to fight back because they know if they don't their inaction might allow serious damage to be done to God's cause. We live in times where the Christians have too many very weak leaders and there is much confusion."

Raf is very thoughtful then asks: "And do too many bad people pray for the wrong things?"

Cautiously: "It is more that their prayers don't come from their hearts. When people come to me to listen to what I say I never offer to pray. That is very personal, and I think people do much better if they pray in private. But that is the way I feel. That is why this is no longer a normal Church. I know some people who visit and sit in silence by themselves to pray, and I would like them to do that. When Paul was alive he said Christianity meant having groups of people meeting to talk about things. He was trying to spread the news of what had happened to him on the road to Damascus and he was right. Today the Christian Church in this country is suffering because the culture of spreading news has changed. We have television, films and newspapers, but for 24 hours a day lies are thrown to us as entertainment and news."

Raf looks serious. "You are saying the Christians have many enemies in this country and they are not Muslims."

"Yes I think that is fair comment. That is why I think perhaps a time will come when the Muslims and the Christians will come together. I think it is possible because it just needs a couple of likeminded worshippers to be born in the same era. A few different words put into the Koran, and for the same to happen to the Bible to make people understand: God is alive, Jesus is alive, Paul is alive and Mohammed is in all probability also alive. I don't personally know your Mohammed so I can't personally vouch for his whereabouts. God through Jesus, helped by Paul gives me what I need and want from life and I want to share this with every British subject if that is possible. If the time arrives, and I am still around, I will get to know Mohammed better. Perhaps you'll be there to help me."

A thought strikes Raf. "But there are three of you and only one for the Muslims?"

"No – our God and your Allah are the same, and we must all worship in the same way or the churches are wasting everybody's time. But we must not damage the nature of God if we try to achieve this. You must remember that Jesus lived a long time before Mohammed and so did Paul. They were Jews, but it would not surprise me to hear that some of their distant relations were also distant relations of yours."

The front doorbell rings.

As they walk to open it, Ralph says, "But would your God make me a prince like Allah will? My mother is a princess. Allah is great and very powerful. I want to go to my mother and I want to live like a prince."

When he gets to the front door Ralph pauses for a moment before opening it. Jon Singer looks anxiously past Ralph to the boy who lifts his left hand in a silent greeting. Jon steps inside and takes a deep breath as he stares straight at Raf. "I was worried about you."

"And I was waiting for my father," is the immediate reply. "He still has not come home. I decided to come to this church because that was the only way I knew how to make contact with you."

Ralph holds the door open and says: "And on that note I will leave the two of you briefly because I have to visit an old friend of mine to see if all is well. That will give you two time to talk."

He leaves and shuts the door behind him.

CHAPTER FIVE

As the door shuts Jon looks at Raf, standing expressionless with both hands in trouser pockets. He asks cautiously, "Do you know where your father is?"

Raf shrugs his shoulders: "With friends. He told me where he was going."

"Has this happened before? When he goes to visit friends does he stay away for several days?"

Raf nods. "They have very important things to talk about. Back home this happens all the time. It is not easy for Palestinians to live normally and to earn money. He does not always tell me where he is going or how long he will be. Have you talked to him?"

Jon shakes his head, "No. I can't phone him, he has to phone me."

Raf's voice does not waiver, "If there is trouble do you think he will phone you?"

Jon is hesitant. "There has been trouble at a house in North London. The police raided a house. There was shooting. Do you know the address where your father went?"

"No. I went with him once but I do not know where it is or how to get there. Was anyone killed?"

His voice remains steady and his eyes expressionless.

Jon nods: "A young boy of about 16 has been shot."

Raf's jaw drops slightly but he waits before saying: "I know him. We met. That is the house where my father went." For a moment he looks small and forlorn. Then he takes his hands from his pockets, turns, and walks several steps away from Jon before stopping. When he turns to face him again his body appears tense. "My mother has always warned me there will be a day when he might not come back. Do you know what has happened to him?"

"The police won't release any further information, Raf. That probably means they are looking for those that got away."

"How many did not get away?"

"Three are in prison, and two were shot. I don't have any details about any of the others except for the young boy."

Raf walks away from him as he says: "But I do have a strong contact at the police who I can phone but when I spoke to him earlier there was still no further information about the identity of the others. Do you know how your father might be identified? He told me he does not have a passport. Do you know if that is the truth? He also said you don't have one either. News always leaks out to some of the journalists. I am hopeful we will soon have more details. Do you know how many were at the meeting?"

Raf turns towards him. "There were ten but you must not tell the police. None of them have passports. My father said that is the best way. But I do not know what I must do next. That is why I came here."

Jon is taken aback. The boy clearly needs his help. He says softly: "I am your friend."

Raf nods and his hand once again digs deep into his lumber-jacket pockets.

"What will you do if your father does not come back?"

"Will you help me? I do not have any money. When will I be able to draw money from the bank?"

Jon is thoughtful, then says: "It will take another day, maybe two? How do you want me to help you?"

"If I can get back to France maybe I can get back to Palestine."

Jon looks relieved: "That I can certainly promise you I'll do. It is much easier to help people get out of this country than into it. Not many normal Englishmen want to emigrate to France."

He watches intently as the boy walks into the gym, chooses a pair of gloves, puts them on, looks carefully as he makes two fists and then proceeds to pummel the heavy bag slowly and repeatedly eventually increasing the speed relentlessly. The sudden explosion of pent-up frustration and anguish, coming from such a frail looking boy surprises Jon who watches with utter fascination until the flailing arms slow down.

Sweat pours from his face as he stops and his arms drop limp down his sides.

Jon sounds cautious: "Do you think the police might be looking for you?"

His heart takes a small jump as the boy turns swiftly and anxiously to him. "You said you are my friend. Did you tell anyone about me?"

Jon immediately shakes his head. "No! no! I have not told anyone anything about you and your father. No one knows you are here. Part of the reason I brought you into the UK was because I thought you could have a better life. And I was going to be the journalist who wrote about it. No one else even has a hint that I had helped you through Customs. Do you know what a scoop means?"

"You are the first one!"

"Right now the police are wondering what was going on at that address, and how many got away, and how many others there are, and what the meeting was all about? What sort of business did your father go and discuss with his friends? I'm asking this only because I want to look after you until I take you back, not for any other reason. If I understand what is going on I will be able to look after you so much easier and better. There is the problem the police might now watch the air and seaports and be much more vigilant about checking cars and so on. I need to know what to expect so that I can plan better."

"It was business for Allah and my father has to go back. If he cannot then I must go back."

"How important was it?"

"Very. That is why ten people went. Everyone had a job to do. Work for Allah is the most important thing I can do, and what my father can do. I was going to earn a lot of money. We need money back home."

"And was you father going to earn a lot of money as well? Do you know what sort of work he is doing?"

"Yes of course. I have said, it is work for Allah. It is complicated. You will not understand. You are not a Muslim."

"So it is work for the Muslims?"

"Yes. I am not allowed to talk about it. Not even to a friend. This is private family business and you won't understand."

Cautiously, Jon persists. "Do you know the people your father went to meet?"

"Yes I met them. They wanted to meet me."

Jon breathes deeply. "And what do you want to do now?"

Raf hesitates and shrugs his shoulders. "I am thinking. I don't know."

"What about the place where you and your father stayed. Won't they help?"

"There is a woman but she has gone and she said if she is not back I must speak to you, because you are the only friend I have."

Jon sounds tense. "That sounds a bit drastic. It's better you don't go back to this house. Trust me. I want to help you but I'm not sure how at this stage. I'll talk to Ralph. This is a very good place for you stay until we know what our plans are, but I don't know if he'll agree to that."

"He is a good man."

"Yes, but some people are not prepared to get involved with other people's problems."

"But that is what he is doing now. He is visiting an old person to see if he's OK. Even my Imam does not do that. You have to go to him, even if you are dying."

Jon decides against replying.

Both are startled as the front door opens and Ralph returns. He looks at the sweaty face of Raf and asks: "Did you enjoy it?"

The boy nods thoughtfully saying, "I feel good."

"And I was able to get away quicker. There was another visitor at the same time."

"Do you do this often?" Jon asks.

"I have a few friends I check on once a week – people who were parishioners at this church and some of whom still drop in to see me. It is the only task I have set myself. I have the time and I enjoy it even if some of them can't stop nattering from the moment I walk in. She's an expert on tabloids and usually approves of what you write about. Are there any further developments?"

Jon shakes his head and hesitates before looking straight at the older man.

"I need to discuss this with you, but before we do I'll give my contact a call to see if he has heard anything?"

The two men both look at Raf who is busy removing the gloves. Ralph says: "The bathroom is at the back. Have a shower. There are clean towels." As the boy walks away he turns to Jon: "I'm guessing you're going to tell me this boy should not go back to wherever he lives. I don't know anything about your circumstances but I suspect you would not want to be seen arriving at your flat with this boy in your company, and if you're hoping there is a place for him to stay here, there certainly is. I have an extension at the back of the church with a bathroom and two bedrooms, and of course, there is all this. But my condition to allow this is that you stay here as long as he has to. I can tell you now that I suspect you are in serious trouble with this boy and the sooner you sort it out the better. If you learn that Raf's father was planning terrorist acts in this country you will have to inform the police whatever the impact that may have on your life. I will not testify against you, but I do not wish to be dragged into this."

Jon looks stunned by the statement and splutters, "I have told him I am prepared to drive him back into France or as far as I can into Europe. If need be I'll take holiday time to make sure he gets back to Palestine, which is where I think he wants to go."

"I will start making the necessary arrangements on the assumption that this is what I am going to have to do. Raf has accepted that this looks like the only thing left for him to do. But he does want to withdraw the money he earned working for me, and that might take two days. I hope that you can put up with us for that long?"

He is aware the older man looks closely at him before he says deliberately. "Why is it I have the impression you know more about this than you're telling me? I do accept you may have been duped into bringing father and son into the UK, but is it too much to expect you to tell me what you know and what exactly is going on? What is your relationship with this boy and do you know how Raf is connected with events in North London?"

Jon splutters. "I give you my word, whatever that is worth to you, that I had chatted to them on a friendly basis as a journalist after his father had offered to give me a guided tour of all the tricky bits around the West Bank and elsewhere – places where he guaranteed many of the Palestinians were prepared to die for their cause. I did not trust him but it was an irresistible opportunity for background information. He promised not to take me anywhere that might put my life at risk. I saw them five times on the West Bank and spent one whole day with them. Raf seemed interested in my job and we became friends. The two said they would give anything to move to the UK, and from that I got the idea to smuggle them in as evidence just how easy it is for illegal immigrants too get into the UK. I arranged to meet them at the Arc de Triomphe, never expecting that they would be there. Four days later I arrived and to my astonishment there they were and I had no idea how they got there. I immediately hired a car. We talked and they convinced me they were homeless thanks to Israeli bombs and were desperate to start a new life. He mentioned he had friends somewhere in London that had emigrated years back and wanted to look them up. He also promised they would assist in helping me to write about Palestine providing they could maintain their anonymity. Journalists don't have to disclose their sources of information. I even had plans for a book about this."

As he pauses for breath Ralph interrupts: "And when did you discover there was a sinister alternative to their plans?"

"When the father started being secretive and started putting off plans for a lengthy in depth interview and introducing me to some of his friends. He did not even want me to know exactly where they lived. So I started building up my relationship with the boy and he seemed keen to earn some pocket money. A wonderful chance to help him came when I was tipped off about some photographs. On this day on the West Bank Raf demonstrated his agility to climb in through the smallest windows of homes."

"I was told by my contact at Scotland Yard that they suspect that there is a woman involved. One of the dead men had a photograph and also a return ticket to Parsons Green. I suspect that is the woman Raf and his father stayed with and I'm very worried his father is one of the two men that were shot."

"Does Raf have any living family?"

"Who knows? We have never discussed it."

Ralph frowns: "I need to think this through. As I've said, Raf can stay but so must you. And you had better discuss taking leave with your editor."

Jon looks trapped: "I'll finish the story I'm writing and talk to the editor. I'm due for some leave, and I think I can talk him into it. What about if I give my friends who were with me the other night a call? Does it have to be me?"

"I can't suddenly put up seven people. And yes, you are necessary. If I am to get further involved I will want to be kept informed about developments. I do not want terrorists knocking on my front door. Now start organising yourself while I see how Raf is getting on."

Jon dials a number on his mobile as Ralph walks towards back of the church.

Several hours later – Ralph faces the small gathering seated in comfortable chairs and looking expectantly at him. Raf is barely visible in his huge chair. Next to him is Jon and on the other side Marion followed by Elizabeth and Peter.

Ralph says thoughtfully, "What a difference a day makes! I'll leave it to Jon to explain the details. Having Rafael as a guest is not a problem for me, and I suggest should not be a problem for any of you."

"Paul never commented on wars and about the problems of an occupying force – as you know the Romans ruled in Israel. In fact he sounded almost compliant in his approach, and we know why. Paul did not comment on a number of things, which we may find extraordinary. But then, he did not set himself up as an author and he understood that life in the flesh, as he liked to refer to it, was sometimes a million miles removed from life in the spirit. Neither did he show all that much interest in the details of life – his main concern was about afterlife. Which is curious, because as a Pharisee his arguments and discussions must have been about existing Jewish culture. The 613 laws of the Torah are exactly that. And after his Experience and his complete turn-around, he was relentless in explaining to people that the New Covenant with God through Jesus was all about afterlife, and the way to achieve this was to think differently, doing things differently, and if they were able to do this it would lead to the first contact with the Kingdom of God."

"In order to spread the word of the new Gospel he set up communities, ministries, to help him, and in order to do this Paul was forced to become involved in the way people lived their lives. They wanted to know, and to be told what they could do and what would prevent them from inheriting life in the presence of God."

"When he first descended on them it was a huge success and those who believed Paul and got caught up in a new life in the Spirit and Paul's Damascus experience found a new freedom lifting them to ecstatic highs. It wasn't just finding release from the Torah, but it was the fact that Paul's Experience virtually guaranteed they would be forgiven their sins. The Resurrection of Jesus and Paul's experience proved there was continuous life. It was an irresistible mixture of good news. But with this success came extra responsibility for Paul. He had to replace the laws of the Torah with new ways of thinking and living, without replacing the old laws simply with a set of new ones, and thereby depriving his Damascus Experience and the story of the Cross of its real meaning. The power of God's Spirit through Jesus provided a wonderful new perspective. Some got so carried away they felt it was as though the New World had arrived and the second coming of Jesus was imminent. Everything felt new and with it came a new quality, a divine quality, a way of hope and charity which had never been experienced before, because it was rooted in God's love and forgiving nature."

"It was an extraordinarily challenging message – how to teach people to live their lives, to work, to have a family and to learn to love the God that had created heaven and earth and everything else, without needing the severe restrictions of the Torah and its consequences of death if one of the laws was breached. Later, after he had matured into a preacher Paul was able to concede that commonsense dictated that some of the old Torah Laws fitted in properly with the New Covenant."

"It wasn't just a time of delivering news – of becoming a part of the only relationship worth cultivating, for his followers it was also a time for learning for Paul. He always spent time wherever he went to make sure his message fitted in with the background of those he addressed."

"In the hundred years before the arrival of Jesus there had been a great expectation of a new world to come, especially among the crushed and desperate people who had no hope for anything else. Paul was brought up to think like this and worship his God in a certain style and sometimes this confuses readers of his letters. But it must be remembered it was his background which inevitably showed through at times, it wasn't a result of what had happened on the Damascus Road."

"Paul grew up believing in a physical resurrection. Most Jews did. As a Pharisee he argued fiercely in protection of this belief. Then followed his Damascus Experience when he was introduced to Jesus by God. He automatically assumed that it was the physical Jesus he had met. At first he never doubted it. That was the news that was handed down by the disciples. When they had heard the tomb of Jesus was empty they also assumed he had been physically resurrected. Jesus appeared to a few very disorientated disciples afterwards but such was the power of these revelations no one tried to establish the exact truth of what they were. There are no recorded discussions of this."

"When Paul recovered from the Damascus Experience and started preaching he ran into difficulties getting people to accept it had been the physical Jesus. But it was only on his visit to Greece that he ran into serious opposition from his hosts that Jesus had been physically resurrected. The Greeks argued against it. They liked the story of the Loving Forgiving God and his resurrected Son, but they did not accept that he had been physically accepted into heaven. This disagreement prevented Paul from establishing a Christian community in Greece."

"It is in reality such an irrelevant point it is amazing how it has remained a worrying and confusing element of the Christian faith through the centuries."

"There is no mystery about the death on the cross of Jesus."

"There is no mystery about the resurrection of Jesus and his appearance to some of the disciples as well as Paul."

"There is no mystery about the empty tomb of Jesus. He did not need his physical body to enter into the presence of his Father."

"There is no mystery about Jesus being the Icon of Christian faith and there is no mystery about Paul's experience on the road to Damascus."

"This made him a witness of God's forgiving nature and power. He was in a position to say with all the confidence and authority of someone who had 'been there and seen and heard it in person' that God was such a magnanimous God He had forgiven Paul for having been the persecuting monster before he was given understanding of the error of his ways. Paul knew that if it had not been for Jesus he would never had learnt the truth about life."

"Jesus was crucified in order to establish life was continuous. He was able to appreciate that the death of Jesus, and the introduction to him in the next life, was acknowledgement that God had forgiven him his sins. But it meant more than that – it gave Paul the divine licence to tell people they could share in his Damascus experience and inherit continuous life if they could muster the faith to do it. This is the Truth of the Christian faith."

"Jesus appeared to the few afterwards to deliver solace to their grieving natures. But there was no specific Ascension Day; Jesus was already in the presence of his Father."

"It took a while for Saul to fully understand the realities of his Experience, and then, such was the joy that he had been singled out and trusted to spread the new word that he changed his name."

"Saul the Pharisee, and persecutor of Christians became the committed apostle Paul attempting to overcome a massive opposition of barbaric wills to appreciate that his God was also their God, and that he was an amazingly caring and forgiving God, and that Jesus, his crucified son was now very much alive and living near his father, very close-by and if only they would believe this and introduce his ways into their daily lives, they could inherit the right to be drawn into His presence when their time arrived."

"It is not known when Paul finally accepted that he would have to abandon his own body when his time was up, but it remained a problem for him for some time. He had been such a close witness to the power of God; he found it difficult to comprehend how the physical aspect of life would eventually become so totally irrelevant to the Creator. It was the final remnant of his early misguided way of believing, and as he matured into the messenger about living a life in the Spirit, Paul converted himself and achieved the spiritual fulfilment he so wanted for all his followers. He was able to explain about the new Covenant with God to the people of the world, and he was able to confirm without any shadow of a doubt that the time would come for them to abandon their bodies for them to be drawn into the presence of God, where they would meet Jesus through whom they have been forgiven their sins."

"It fitted together perfectly. Paul had been reborn to become living proof that Jesus was alive and that God's grace would assist all those who wanted to join his presence in continuous life."

"Sometimes Paul's choice of words sound like a riddle. He liked to talk about living in the flesh, but he conceded it was possible to live a devout life in the cause of the Almighty while enjoying normal things like eating, drinking and having normal relations with women. It was all part of God's nature. For him people who had not yet been in touch with living in the Spirit – those who were still outside the Kingdom of God that Jesus spoke about, were the ones in danger of losing out. They were the threatened ones, living in constant peril, cut off from the truth and what it offered them, and leaving them having to cope with a grim bleak future on their own. He spoke in opposite terms, because when it came to death there were two choices only – there was no escape for those who tried to be neutral."

"It gave their lives very disturbing boundaries, and it left them weak and very vulnerable in the presence of all kinds of demons and hostile powers. Some were forced to seek relief in strange religious practices but these invariably proved pointless and without any sustaining power."

"Death was seen as the inexorable end to life and completely the opposite of life in the Spirit. Relationships are what gives life its meaning and substance, and life with God through Jesus whom Paul could vouch for is alive and well, and provided adherents with their only chance of continuous life in the presence of God."

"At the time when Paul spent his longest spell in prison, and he wrote to friends saying, any day he expected to be told he had been sentenced to death, yet he was still able to proclaim, that for him death would be 'a gain'."

"I have explained to Raf that this must not be confused with current problems in different parts of the world where some very bad leaders are setting themselves up as religious gurus and promising followers untold riches in heaven for martyrdom. None of us know what God's plans are for us, and if we deliberately allow ourselves to interfere fatally in the lives of those around us, under the misguided promise that we will be richly rewarded in the next life, we will in fact instead be confronted by the most horrendous shock of our lives."

"Paul saw that death had no power over Jesus, and when he felt free enough to admit that death held no threat for him, he said it to his followers. That was his driving force, his biggest wish, to get people to see that death can be defeated. That was the Spirit of the Damascus Road Experience. It meant being in the presence of God through Jesus. If we take Jesus and Paul away from our worship we might as well worship rocks and trees, and if we deny that Jesus is alive and near God, then the Christian faith would be nothing more than degraded politics."

"There are many people living in today's very sophisticated cultures who refuse to even try to understand, but this is their problem. There are equally many who try to tamper and even change the nature of God, but the folly they will heap upon their hopes for salvation will be devastating."

"God does not expect miracles or heroic deeds from everyone. Many are born meek and weak but their faith will empower them when their time on earth is over. If your thinking is totally controlled by what you do and how you live then you haven't a hope of ever getting into a receptive mode to enable the power and love of God to enter into your life."

"Paul was an inspirational leader. He sought to liberate people from their old self. A new life, a new experience for the community in which they live."

"For some during those hectic early days it caused many problems, because the new freedom they felt from Paul's experience was that they thought it gave them rights to do what they liked. This really offended Paul, particularly when it put his own life under the spotlight. There is no mention what had happened to the wife of Paul, but he explained that for him a celibate life had become the most natural way to exist. Thinking, living and working for God brought a celibate state of mind which was preferable and totally acceptable for him."

"This underlined his radical approach to many of the questions he was asked on his travels. He always insisted in getting down to the most basic essentials. Paul was forever considering and trying to find the right words to explain God's salvation, and it always centred on the nature of God. But he was also a wonderful optimist, a bit of a poet and he simply could not resist an opportunity to sing the praises of the God who had plucked him from the jaws of self destruction on the road to Damascus."

"This Experience had given Paul the gift of being totally open-minded and very close to the presence of God whenever he wanted to be in communication."

"It enabled him to shut out whatever else was happening around him, and it remained as the main source of his inner strength and commitment. Only Elijah, an Old Testament prophet, is said in the Bible to have had the same gift."

"The details of the Crucifixion of Jesus and the aftermath must not be seen as a problem for believers. At the time it was the most devilish way to illustrate man's inhumanity to man. To kill a man like Jesus in such a barbaric manner scales the heights of brutality, but such acts are often repeated today for political and other selfish ends."

"When God gave humans a free will he knew he faced a very difficult, if not impossible task to receive assistance from them to achieve his grand design. The story of the Cross was not allowed to take place just to allow mankind to discover there is indeed continuous life, it also demonstrates that the way we die is accepted by our Maker and he has the power to cope with it, for each and every individual."

"Paul describes it perfectly when he says, by dying we become alive in a new way near God and in his presence. It may sound simple and straightforward, but such are the gifts from God. They form part of a new world but they are in reality very straight-forward. Judgement day is not the image we have of God on his throne, Jesus next to him, and all the saints in evidence. It is in reality quite easy to understand, and swift because it has to be. Contact with God's presence must be maintained if continuous life is to be come a reality."

"Jesus may only have appeared to very few individuals after his crucifixion, but such was the power of this divine Truth, it resulted into millions of believers scattered all over the world of today. God has not revealed his Grand Design for creating earth, but those who are drawn into his presence will know they are part of it."

"The detractors of the Christian Faith say the Resurrection should have manifested before a large crowd. No one would have doubted it then. But no one who has made contact with life in the Spirit doubts it now!"

"Paul's experience took God's message a step further. He was the baddy who became a goody, and he had been a persecutor and prosecutor of Christians. We don't have all the details, but it is written that Paul stood by and watched as James was stoned to death by other Christian persecutors. Paul refers to the monster he was before God drew him into his presence."

"Because of his Jewish background, upbringing and the depressing times they lived in, Paul, came to the wrong conclusion several times after his Damascus Experience. Because he had seen the living Jesus he assumed the Second Coming was on its way, and that God was already shaping out the New World most Jews had been expecting for over a hundred years."

"The real message was that Resurrection is an individual thing. That is how it is and has to be. Jesus proves this and it is underlined by the fact that Jesus appeared to individuals only. It cannot happen collectively."

"The manifestation of Jesus to the disciples is not the same as the one experienced by Paul. God drew Paul into his presence, using his immense personal presence to do this. The same power was not in evidence when Jesus appeared to Mary Magdalene, Cephas and others. There was no need. It was an unexpected gift and bonus for those who, through no arrangement of their own, found themselves briefly elevated spiritually to a level that is awarded with this heavenly insight of the world to come."

Ralph pauses, then continues: "Thank you all for coming. We have a very special guest with us in Rafael, who is approaching the rewarding age of 13. Raf, as he is known, has some serious decisions to make very shortly. Jon has offered to drive him back to France, in the same way he was brought here. Our thoughts will be with Raf all the way on his journey. There is hope that the war will end soon, but even then it will take a long time for peace to reign. Should he wish to come and visit us again then he will be very welcome, and on a private level I want him to understand that my offer to him remains on the table."

"I decided to continue with my talks about Paul because I could see no better way of dealing with what is a challenge for all of us today."

"Raf is a Muslim, but I have already told him I look forward to a day when Muslims and Christians will worship the same God. I personally can't see why this should be a problem. All it requires are some modifications to the history as it appears to have been recorded and the way the Bible and other similar books are read today. But of course, it may take another hundred years or so. Raf is a strong Muslim with very strong faith in Allah."

"I have told him that Christianity has some anomalies that need sorting out, just as the Muslim faith has. I would have liked to have spent some time with him to discuss subtle but inconsequential differences between the two religions, and who knows, he might have developed into a powerful link between the two. He is like no other boy any of us have known, and if he could have left believing that the new Palestine needs people who believe every individual must be a prophet for peace, living in harmony with its arch-enemy, then his visit to us will have been really worthwhile. This country is far from perfect but we do know how to rub along with the bad, the ugly and the selfish. In order to play a major role he must stay alive and help his friends to do the same."

"For every Palestinian that could be the first knock on the door to the real Kingdom of God. From now on he must learn to make his own decisions. Right now he intends to return to his own country. In the same situation perhaps all of us would have chosen to do the same. Raf still feels a commitment to how things were for him when he first arrived in this country. We can only assure him there is a freedom in the world that will help him to find his release from that commitment. Even at his age he must learn to find the strength within himself to look for it. All we can do is to ask God to inspire him and to help him to find a new direction. There is a new life available for Raf but he needs to recognise it himself. Should he choose to stay here he will be very welcome to stay with my wife and myself, and we will not insist on him doing anything except to spend a bit of time to give his mind a chance to relax."

"He has been here in the UK with his father on business, but I suspect that the business has not been successful and Raf now has to decide what is the best way forward for him."

"I have already discovered that he enjoys hitting the punch-bag, and there are other machines to challenge him. Of course, if he decides to stay here for a period I will need help. I have a wife who lives in our other house and she is very involved as warden with her local church. We are not separated in any sense, but each of us is doing our own thing for God. I will have to draw her into the deal. If Raf would like to extend his visit, and if he wants to I will arrange for schooling, I regret to say. He is so grown up already, and a survivor of a very pernicious and nasty war in Palestine. He may feel it is step backward to return to a school, and that is where all of us can help. If he wants to there is a lot he can learn and enjoy doing with us."

"But he is still a boy and I would wish him to enjoy the life of a boy. There are many very exciting things for him to do, should he become interested. I think I know what to tell him is available, but the decision will be his. Should he choose to stay I would want all of you to remain involved in some way. He is our friend. The technicalities of him remaining in London will have to be approached and I think Jon and I can take care of that."

"The whereabouts of Raf's father is unknown but Jon has some resourceful contacts and in due course we will know more about this."

"There are enough beds here for everyone to stay the night. I hope you are all able to do so. I think Raf will prefer to be on his own and I will make a bed for him in this main room, perhaps near the gym in case he wants to avail himself at any time."

"This is a new development for myself and I am prepared to discuss every step we take with everyone present. As things stand at this moment, Raf is planning to be driven back to France tomorrow or the next day, depending when Jon can find the time."

"I am sure you all appreciate that plain speaking is essential, especially from Raf. Paul often used imagery, and thoughts that seems to test the things we see as normal and straightforward. Sophistication can bring knowledge as well as grave danger. But we must reassure Raf that doubt at this stage of his life is very normal and very healthy if he openly talks about it. All of us here have the ability to reassure him, whatever problem he thinks he has. We have the feminine touch, Jon has access to an important newspaper, and Peter wants to go to war for the Christians – not against the Muslims, but all the liars and hate salesmen and the politicians and television producers who are deliberately trying to change the character of the people and their Christian faith, because ultimately they think that is the best way to get their own political demands accepted. We have even had a president who argued about the meaning of the word 'is'. Truth gets abused very often because people's minds are locked into their own little worlds."

"Paul's achievements are amazing, because they came at a time when so little was known about the God who created the earth, and heavens and all the people on it. On top of it all, he is an invisible God. Paul wanted to open up people's minds to be closer to God, because he knew that this gift would be controlled by an appreciation of the power of God and would therefore make them immune to the wrong sort of propaganda."

"Most people do accept the need for the church and for a time when minds must be elevated to contemplate spiritual life. The need for the real Jesus and his friend Paul was great and still remains. And 650 years after their time Mohammed based his religion on the same God and also some of the history. If only he had managed to understand the true nature of God."

"Paul's courage, commitment and gratitude to the God who was prepared to forgive him for his previous life, was unbelievable in modern terms. Paul never forgot this and he never lost his humility when some of his followers heaped praise on him. He always said he had carried out the work of God and could never have done it without Him controlling his actions and words."

"And that in itself caused many divisions on his travels. Paul was accused by his countrymen of being a traitor and many simply wrote off the idea of God choosing the crucifixion to bring about salvation, while those who were already looking for more meaningful lives felt a wonderful new power working within themselves."

"It was the awakening of the Spirit within and at the same time, discovering that God has his own world and that he will allow some of us to enter that world – even those who died the most horrible deaths."

~ ~ ~ ~ ~

It is several hours later and after midnight. Ralph is aware that the light in the gym where Raf was in bed was still on. It doesn't surprise him as he had given the boy permission to let it remain on all night if he wished.

He eases out of bed and reaches for a gown.

As he enters the room he sees Raf sitting on the bed with knees pulled up under his chin. He is still fully dressed.

After a moment he turns round walks into the kitchen and switches the light on. He also fills the kettle and starts preparing to make a hot drink.

After a few minutes Raf joins him.

"I'm making hot chocolate . Perhaps this will help you to relax and get to sleep."

"But I don't want to sleep," the boy says softly. "It is my last night and I want to be awake. I like your home, your church and the other things as well. I am asking my mother to tell me what to do next?"

"Your stay has been very brief Raf. I have talked a lot to you because of this. I hope you will remember some of the things I told you."

"I will remember a lot, perhaps everything if I try hard. I like this man Paul and I am happy that you know him so well. What I don't understand is why Christians and Muslims can't pray side by side."

Ralph hands him a mug.

"In Paul's time, before he had this wonderful experience, there was no real religion. People used the same old prayers over and over and these prayers were mostly for the people who were very poor and also poor in their minds. They tried to cheer themselves by praying and hoping that God would reward them with riches in the next life. Some created their own Gods."

"Jesus was first to tell people what Heaven and Paradise really is all about, later Paul was able to confirm that that was the truth. God introduced Paul to Jesus, to show him he was alive and very well. That started something new. Jesus and Paul were the first human beings to become part of a new world. They helped to open the Kingdom of God on earth and show people how to progress into the next life, by thinking differently, doing different things, living differently and praying to the one God, who loved all his people and who was a very caring and generous God."

The boys voice trembles. "And what about my mother?"

"She will always be your princess Raf. It is right you think like that. She was a good woman, and she worried about you, and she wanted you to be with Allah."

Raf's voice drops to a whisper: "There were days when she did not eat because she did not want me to be without food. She needs me to be with her. I can feel that strongly. And I have things I want to tell her. Good things she does not know."

Ralph replies gently, "I can't see any reason why you won't meet up with her, Raf. God is a very generous to those who love him and it sounds to me as though you are ready to learn quickly how to do this really well. It is the most important law of all. If you can learn to love your Creator properly, then everything else you do will be thoughtful and your judgement will be brilliant."

"But I have loved him for a long time", is the boy's swift reply. "I always said my prayers even when I did bad things. There are many things I did not understand, but because my father and the Imam told me to do them I did. A son must listen to his father. Who else can he listen to?"

"I can't argue with that Raf, except to say that God is your father and mine. Jesus showed us that suffering will not prevent anyone from inheriting the next life, and I promise you the riches you will find while in the presence of God are beyond all your expectations and understanding right now. But I think you are beginning to appreciate that the leaders of both our countries, political and religious, have a lot of very hard work to do before they acquire the wisdom to solve some of our problems. Trouble is most politicians are atheists or at best agnostic."

"One of the big problems for Christians today is that life is so good for them, they have lost touch with God's righteousness. They think because they give to the poor, and because they fawn over the rights of misguided minority groups that all is well for them, but such is the pleasure and love they feel for themselves that they fail to recognise that God's love and pleasure does not reach out for them."

"Those who do not look for God in this life, will have no chance of finding him in the next. I can feel the anxiety and stress in you and I want to help but only if you want me to. Palestine is very different from England but I wish things would settle down in your country because I have a desire to visit it. And I want you to be there so that you can be my guide."

"You must take care, stay alive, and become a leader for your people and tell them their God must be the same God as ours, but this can only happen if the true nature of God is number one for everyone. You have the passion and the need to be close to your God, because you also want to be close to your mother. Love is at the heart of all our expectations and you may be blessed in discovering that loving your God is the greatest and most fulfilling love of all. If you join your mother at the end of a successful and productive life, you will discover exactly what I have said to you. I think for you that could be a truly wonderful discovery. And it does not mean you must give up everything else that you have to do, like having a job, and helping to look after your family, and supporting your friends. The war has closed your mind to what life could be like Raf."

"No one felt stronger about this than Paul who often was heard to say he wants to experience what Jesus did and like him he wanted to find himself back again in the presence of God. He knew what it was like and he knew there was nothing else he wanted more than that, because he also knew that is where we meet the ones we love and that also includes Jesus and also Paul. But even though Paul travelled far and wide, and offered his information free, he had many enemies who were frightened because they knew their own way of life was under threat, and many people, when threatened like this want to destroy those they deem to be responsible. But he also had friends, and he managed to stay out of reach of those who tried to kill him. He carried on because he knew that Jesus was alive and that this message had the power to stay alive forever."

"Paul became the first man to receive a saving revelation direct from God when he was introduced to Jesus. From then on he used all his natural physical and mental strength, his powers of persuasion, and continued divine inspiration to persuade as many people as he could to enter into a new covenant, a relationship with God, and become part of his great scheme for creation. Paul wanted to draw a line under the history of the world and make a new start with everyone involved as part of the people of God. But as you know there is still a lot of work to be done. If you think God is calling you then you must think hard about it. You are young and healthy. You can do a lot of good even if you only become a husband and a father."

He walks the boy back to his bed. Raf stops and then starts unbuttoning his lumber jacket. Ralph is startled when he sees the belt with pockets around Raf's middle but he decides against making any comment. Raf removes it and hangs it over a chair with his jacket lying on the seat. Then, still wearing his trousers, he sits on the edge of the bed. Ralph steps back, lifts his left hand in a greeting and the boy silently does the same.

The following morning, at just after nine o'clock, Jon and Raf drive off with those remaining behind waving their good-byes. Ralph rushes back inside and walks anxiously towards the gym. As he approaches his eyes focus on the belt still hanging on the chair and he stops in his tracks leans against a pillar, breathing very deeply.

Two hours later the telephone rings near the kitchen. He lifts it and Jon's voice crackles softly "We're having a bite to eat in a café in Canterbury. I have been to a bank and drawn money from my own account and I have given Raf his earnings in Euros. I have also just spoken to my contact at the Yard. The return train ticket to Parsons Green makes it look certain Raf's father was the second man killed but I haven't told him yet. I'm not sure if I should do this, because I have no idea how he might react. What do you think?"

Ralph hesitates before saying, "Frankly I don't know. I can see why you feel concerned. But I do have some news. Raf was wearing one of these belts with pockets large enough to be loaded with explosives. He hung the thing over the chair next to his bed, and it is still hanging there. If I was a pessimist I might think he forgot to put it back on, but I doubt that is so. He was surely very much aware of the thing around his waist all the time since you met with them in Paris. What we don't know is if that was the reason for contacting the friends in North London."

"Neither you nor I know anything about the real Raf, except we do know now he must have come here on a mission arranged by his father. What has he been like on the journey to Canterbury?"

"We spoke about you mostly and your gymnasium, and that you offer people free advice."

Ralph chooses his words with care, "Well, I've checked the belt. There are no explosives and, just to make sure, I checked under the mattress. In fact I've carefully looked everywhere in the gymnasium but there is nothing."

"It seems therefore Raf was waiting for his orders from his father, and had he returned from the meeting, he would have brought back the explosives for the belt."

"Or perhaps the woman has a role to play. A woman and a boy would have looked much more incongruous than a man and a boy, especially if the man looked like a street trader. I think you should tell him that it looks as though his father may have been the second victim of this raid, but be prepared for any or every eventuality. He doesn't look dangerous, but there you are. He was wearing this belt all the time he was with you. His face is the innocent mask of Palestine."

Silence, then: "This is exactly what I feared. I don't know if I'm going to have the courage to tell him. I'll let you know when we're closer to Dover."

"My contact also told me they found a list of names – all highly prominent politicians. Next to the names there is data about their whereabouts for the next ten days, and there are also large sums of money against the names."

A very restless Ralph spends the next 30 minutes again carefully searching every nook and cranny of the nave. When he doesn't find anything he kneels against the bed for spiritual sustenance.

The phone interrupts sharply and he walks swiftly to it. Jon says softly:

"I think Raf wants to take you up on your offer. We're on our way back."

Part Two

Chapter Six

Ralph frowns as he replaces the phone. Normally he enjoys a quick chat with Sheila, who has to spend her remaining days in a wheelchair, but on this occasion he really wanted to talk to her son, and he is away helping out a friend with his fruit stall in the market.

Nothing normally catches him off guard, but Jon Singer's call that he was bringing back Raf has knocked him sideways. He has always semi-prepared himself for the unexpected, and unpredictable, or even bad news but this was definitely unexpected. It will take some time before he will know exactly what sort of news it turns out to be. The redeeming aspect of this new development is that he already likes the boy and believes they should get on.

Life, however, will never be the same again, even if the stay was only for a short period. The boy is an illegal immigrant, smuggled into the country by a top journalist. Although it wasn't spelt out in so many words, Raf is also a potential suicide bomber, with links to some of those living in this country with similar catastrophic ambitions.

His reaching for the phone to speak to Travis was not only instinctive, but almost feverish. Sheila's son is ex-MI5, invalided from the force after being on the receiving end of a half dozen bullets during an earlier shoot-out with a gang of would be terrorists. Aged 36 he is now trying to rebuild his life with his body covered in scars after five bullets had made a devastating mess of his left shoulder and left knee.

He shakes his head in disbelief that he had spoken so glibly to such a young person about a matter that could have such serious consequences for so many different individuals. Helping him to discover a new God is one thing, but having to cope with the mess of laws and regulations they will have to fight through before that boy can become the recipient of a much better future, is a totally different and daunting proposition.

This could turn out to be the most rash invitation he has ever extended to anyone.

Feeling edgy and irritated with himself he walks purposefully towards the gym, and as he reaches the heavy bag his right hand uppercut sinks heavily into it and the hall reverberates with a shudder.

Jon Singer had better have some very bright ideas and plans. If he thinks he can simply dump that boy at this address, he is in for a nasty surprise. Surely he must realise there is no way that boy could live here on his own with a man in his fifties. They will have to find foster parents but that will mean Singer will have to own up to having smuggled the boy into the country.

Ralph is unable to stifle a groan as he reaches for a chair. In no time at all he could have the government, the police, the social services and the church authorities accusing him of all kinds of nasty things.

Singer had better be thinking straight about this. Maybe he has a relation prepared to look after the boy? Maybe Raf only wants to extend his stay in the UK for a few weeks? But would that be for a different purpose, a much more sinister purpose? He has his own mobile. Maybe he spoke to someone on the way down to Dover.

All sorts of possibilities flash through his mind, until he calms down as he thinks about the slightly built, pale and always serious looking Raf pounding the punch bag relentlessly. There are demons in him, of that he has no doubt, but he is fairly sure the boy is fighting a personal battle to get rid of them.

And he feels comforted as he recalls Singer saying the boy has decided to opt for the offer of a new life. But weighing heavily against this is the fact that the shoot-out in North London means there is unfinished business and the leaders are still free. Have his Palestinian friends been in touch with him?

As he sits down again, he takes a deep breath and looks around the empty hall. Just as he had thought life would be much smoother from now on a new problem pops up. And having that boy living here must first be treated as a problem, before he can attempt to try and be a help to him.

Travis has done a superb job as builder, adding on two extra rooms with a bathroom behind the chancel, and also renovating the basement and transforming it into a smaller version of the St Martins in the Field basement restaurant. It could also become an independent two bed roomed flat should he wish to use it as such. It is going to be an exciting new addition in the life of this building. It will be a joy to plan extra activities and to utilise all the extra space.

He immediately dispels the thought that God may have other plans for himself. It doesn't work that way or does it? He is never sure. Staying in close touch with his Maker provides him with immense confidence and strength to tackle everything, but he is always aware that he lives in a world dominated by powerful and destructive free wills. And he will hopefully have the help of Travis and other young people who have tried to persuade him to have weekend get-togethers on a regular basis. He'll simply have to work his way through, but it could prove very challenging. The worst part of it is the threat of official red tape. This is where the experience of Travis will be invaluable. If Raf's friends, or former friends are looking for him, Travis is the man he wants at his side.

That is another thing that must be established immediately. How much is the boy in touch with them and do they know what his new plans are and where he will be staying?

Jon Singer will have to pull his weight. There is no way he will be allowed to draw Copsem Gardens into his wild journalistic ambitions. For a start Singer must establish that the boy's father is dead, and it must also be established if Raf is still in contact by phone with any of the remaining would-be terrorists.

It may well be Travis will have to get MI5 involved. If the terrorists need Raf, they will not allow him to slip away.

Chapter Seven

Jon Singer curses beneath his breath as he hears the click that tells him Ralph has hung up. He had expected a different reaction.

Men of God, or is this one a man of Paul, are supposed to be masters in diplomacy, good stiff upper lip graciousness, delivering platitudes that they hope will soothe the sinner. Some welcome with open arms the challenge to fight for the soul of what could be deemed a lost cause.

As he arrives at a stretch of road free of oncoming traffic he casts a sideways glance at the boy, who in turn, continues to stare straight ahead, almost as though he had not heard himself speaking to Ralph.

"You are sure this is what you want," and then he adds swiftly, "it's the most important decision of your life."

Raf makes him wait for his reply, "He did say Allah and your God are almost alike?"

"Umm, yes. That is what baffles most intellectual people in the west. But you had better discuss this with him. He seems to know all the answers. All I know is that your Mohammed married the daughter of an English vicar. She probably helped him borrow some ideas from Jesus. It's that close. Women are very ingenious the way they influence the men they are married to. All this nonsense you've been reading about women getting equal rights, is the biggest mistake they have ever made. Just think about it. Women have physically always been the weaker sex. They have always needed and wanted to be looked after but they have brains just as good, and sometimes better than the men they marry. So they manage them, very cleverly, because men always just want a peaceful time, food on their table, and a couple of other things. Now some women have turned themselves into bossing freaks, and the men won't marry them anymore, because they will lose everything they own, if the women decide to leave them. This is just one of the disasters our chameleon

Prime Minster has introduced to mess up what used to be a fairly contented land. When you live here you'll find yourself becoming more interested in politics. It's your democratic right. Don't ever forget that."

"It is the same in Palestine."

"Really?"

"Of course, the Americans have taught us."

"And us too," Singer hears himself saying.

Then it strikes him. Something about this boy has worried him ever since he has met him. He has never seen him smile. But he knows now is not the time to try and change that.

Has Ralph noticed this as well? What exactly is this man, who seems to know an ancient prophet as though he is a best friend, thinking at this very moment? Is he happy about the prospect of Raf moving in with him? That's how it will have to be. There is no way he could have Raf sharing his two roomed flat. His landlady would have a fit, and so would all his friends.

And it was Ralph who offered this new life to a boy who seemed to be hurtling lemming-like towards a horrifying extinction. No one can blame Raf for grabbing a lifeline. If that is really what he wants? What kind of force is it that persuaded him to want to sacrifice his young life in this way? It really is going to be the most challenging threat to resolve and it may indeed land him in prison, and sacked from his job.

And yet when the boy said he wanted to stay, his heart took a gigantic leap. It felt like an extraordinary achievement, until harsh reality set in. From now on he will be worrying every moment of the day about being exposed as a terrorist sympathiser. What had possessed him to bring this boy to the UK? He had walked into a trap –a devastating terrifying trap created by himself. He has no one but himself to blame for not thinking beyond writing a story and then handing this boy over to the authorities. That may still be the only way to handle this.

He casts his eyes sideways to look at the small hunched figure. What is he thinking about? Does he have the thoughts of a young conniving conman, like his father? Or is he in fact a genuine Muslim with only one thing in mind, to join his mother in her palace in paradise? Inadvertently his foot eases on the accelerator and the car gently stops as he drives into a lay-by. The London lights form a massive encouragement for many people without hope. He is aware of Raf looking expectantly at him.

"As I was paying for the petrol I noticed you were on the phone? Did someone call?" He knew that Raf probably only ever used the mobile to speak or receive calls from his father and also the woman with whom they stayed. Was she also involved with this gang? If so she will be concerned about his whereabouts. Has she called?

Raf again fixes his stare on the road ahead: "I tried to phone Lilah at the house where I was staying but there was no answer. I have to tell her what I'm doing. I have known her most of my life. She will need to know."

Singer feels his blood curdling cold and his voice drops an octave as he says: "Can we first talk to Ralph before you make any further calls. He may not want your friends to know that you will be staying with him."

Raf's reply is immediate: "I will not tell them. I know what you're saying."

Singer feels reprimanded, and asks gently "It sounds as though you appreciate there are difficulties that must be faced and resolved if you are to stay in this country."

"I know. The law says I'm an illegal asylum seeker. I don't mind that. I see you as my friend and you will know what to do. I also trust this man who owns the church. There is not anything I can do for myself at this stage, so I wait for you and him to tell me what is to happen to me. But if I don't like what you say, then I want to go back to Palestine. I have some money, I will pay for you to take me back again if that is how it is."

Singer silently nods his agreement. Then decides to probe a bit further.

"Are you worried something may have happened to Lilah. Did she go with your father?"

There had been no report about the presence of a woman from the police and Singer knew neither of the victims was reported to have been a woman.

"I don't know," Raf says.

"Does she have your number?"

"Of course."

"Is she a relation?"

"She's a friend from Palestine. We grew up together. She came here some months ago."

Singer decides to venture further.

"Which means she rented a house or flat?" he asks nonchalantly. Raf shrugs his shoulders, but Singer immediately knows she has to be connected with the network operating in the UK. Before he can stop himself he asks: "What made you decide to stay?"

Again Raf's voice reveals no emotion. "I have nothing to go back to. My grandparents and my parents are dead. I have one cousin and she is married to a member of Hamas. Soon she will be dead as well. I like the man in the church and I like his gym, and you paid me £2000 to climb through a window and bring you a picture. I think I should stay here and see what happens."

Singer is aware the boy is looking at him for a response. "I know in the past when I tried to persuade you to come to the UK, I said that living under a democracy such as ours, is the best way to live. But don't be misled, we have a lot of problems in this country but I think even the most angry beggar, searching the streets for food every day, will agree we all have a right to our own opinion, and if we don't like what the other person says or thinks, we agree to disagree. But you're going to have to prepare yourself for testing times ahead."

Outside a persistent drizzle is making the car wipers work overtime. Raf says: "I like rain. Where we live we don't see it often and then it's thunder and lightning."

To Singer's surprise there is an empty parking spot outside the lychgate. He is unable to suppress his appreciation.

"Perhaps it is reserved for him." Raf says quietly as he looks at the church. It seems more lit up as though there are extra lights pouring through the windows.

CHAPTER EIGHT

Street markets, wherever they arrive, overnight, be it in parts of bustling cities or small coastal towns always attract extra interest. Tourists flock with curiosity, and the town people look forward to it because they deem it an essential part of business life, especially if they are regular clients. For Travis Duncan his one day stint a week at the market in this particular part of London has acted as therapy, after those terrorist bullets had prematurely ended his highly promising career, first as Detective Inspector for the Met Police and then for MI5 after they had spotted his talent and drawn him into the circle of men who quietly sort out the activities of suspected individuals who might threaten the stability of life in the United Kingdom.

It would take very close scrutiny to spot he has a plastic knee, an almost plastic shoulder, and a plastic ear fitted over part of the original.

During his police career he had spent hours on two occasions scanning the people who attended the market for suspected criminals. When a friend of his, who had his own spot selling high quality fruit and vegetables, and bits and pieces of clothing, told him he needed someone to look after his business while he went to Covent Garden once a week to replenish stocks, he unhesitatingly grabbed the opportunity and offered his help.

He suspected his widowed mother might have had a hand in the offer from his old school friend Richard, but he was all for it. He always enjoyed watching individuals, and even though the people who bought and sold at this market did not represent a cross section of Londoners, it was surprising how many strangers kept popping up fairly regularly.

Like the mysterious Latin looking woman, probably in her early thirties, who totally intrigued and fascinated him. He suddenly spotted her leisurely walking between the stalls, stopping to briefly look at something without ever touching it. She seemed to have a perfect figure and her face and eyes exuded a quiet confidence. To his delight she came straight to him to ask for "mangoes?" The expression on her beautiful face implied she wasn't sure he would understand what mangoes were. Although his body language at the time did not let him down, he searched rather frantically for the fruit, which he knew was kept in a special place for special customers.

Richard supplies unusual African and Indian fruit to his special customers. These are always kept in warmer conditions to ensure maximum flavour. Warmed for a short period ensures the flavour was perfect before he delivered and in this way he built up his reputation.

On this occasion he sold one of the mangoes that had been promised to a regular customer but when Richard heard the story he forgave his friend and promised to have one extra ripe mango on hand in case this wonderful creature ever came back again. She did, almost exactly two weeks later and within a few minutes of ten o'clock, when he normally had a short break for a cup of coffee.

And she arrived as mysteriously as she did previously – from nowhere. As he looked up, there she was, with the same anxious look on the olive skin surrounded by what looked like genuine black hair. When she walked away she seemed in no hurry and he cursed himself for having been so tongue-tied. There must have been something he could have thought of to mention to her. She looked like a tourist. They do sometimes reach this part of London.

Her "thank you" sounded so relieved he only just resisted the temptation of saying: "Its on me luv – especially for you." He placed it in the bag she held in her right hand and, after casting him just the briefest of glances, she slowly walked away.

It was two weeks to the day, and almost 10 am. He wondered if that was pure coincidence or whether there was a reason. And then he saw her again, but this time further away and her body language seemed to say she was looking for, or expecting someone to join her. And then he arrived, his longish black beard covering much of the face from below the nose. Travis wasn't sure whether his furry coat was mink or nylon? It was too far to see.

It was a curious meeting, with neither saying anything at first but then he removed his hand from the coat pocket and handed her something. They chatted briefly and then he nodded with what might have been a smile and both started walking slowly down the middle of the road past people walking just as leisurely in the opposite direction. Travis lowered his eyes, expecting her to walk past his stall but she didn't. Their eyes met and this time he was sure there was a sadness that made him wonder she was perhaps expecting to be told there are no mangoes and she needn't bother to ask. His hand reached to the spot where he knew he had placed the biggest and ripest one and her eyes lit up briefly. The first time and there was just a touch of a smile when he produced the fruit perched on the tip of his fingers before she had said a word.

"This one is from Africa, and I've been told it is a very good tree," he says, attempting to sound nonchalant.

"You make it sound like a special tree. I shall enjoy it even more. Thank you. Same price?"

Her English sounded good, perhaps not perfect, inflected by a touch of Mediterranean.

He nodded. His eyes again locked into hers and she seemed to hesitate for just another lingering moment before turning, again nodding her appreciation, and slowly walking away. The bearded individual had paused in the middle of the road a dozen metres away and half turned to wait for her. But she did not join him so much as wander off in the same direction with him walking a metre in front of her. She only bought one mango, so she was not going to share it with the man with the hair, Travis thought with some satisfaction. He certainly does not look her type he mumbled under his breath.

But there was just a hint of familiarity between them and they probably knew one another well. It was the way he handed her the paper or envelope and the way she had taken it.

Is he a brother, surely not her father, an uncle, a relation, a friend, certainly not a lover? Next time he will try and lure her into conversation. Her thank you today contained a much more personal and familiar touch. She doesn't appear to be in a hurry. Maybe she's looking for a chance to talk to an English person. There definitely was something odd about her relationship with the bearded individual – she had placed the envelope in her bag without opening it or even glancing at it, which meant she probably knew what it was. He felt sure it was a brown envelope. The natural curiosity that had been with him all through his previous careers felt intrigued and he could not wait to see her again. He also knew he might never see her again and her friendliness on this occasion might have been her style of saying goodbye and thanks for the mangoes. If only Richard had been here he would have followed them just to see if they continued to go in the same direction, and perhaps even entered the same address.

But Richard did not return for another hour and when he did get back around midday and listened to Travis he merely said "If this is going to become a habit, then you're going to have to deliver the mangoes from now on, and you're going to have to explain why there is another one short. I don't want my customers to think I'm losing it."

"I've got a feeling she may be Israeli." Travis says thoughtfully: "I once spent a few days in Jerusalem, and I'm convinced she's from that part of the world and I'm willing to wager that bearded guy is not a Londoner."

Richard sounds slightly disgusted: "Yes well, I'm not interested in the bet. You've evidently never stopped thinking about her since you first laid your eyes on her, but now you know there is a man in her life I can tell you one thing for sure. Neither of them are big spenders, and until you tell me she bought all the mangoes at the same time, I am just not interested."

Travis smiles. "At least I know she knows more than two words of English."

Richard reaches for the box with mangoes and groans. "You gave her the biggest and ripest one again. I have an 80 year old lady with only days to live waiting for that one."

That shocked Travis. His own mother is that age.

Richard is amused by his response. "Forget it, I was only kidding. I suppose if it only happens every two weeks I can live with it."

Three further customers arrive and then another two simultaneously, as though they knew he had just brought fresh produce.

The mobile in the pocket of Travis gives a few sharp rings and he quickly steps back and takes it from his pocket. It is his mother telling him that Ralph wants to see him today, as soon as he has time.

Chapter Nine

The kitchen table comfortably accommodates six people. Singer at first felt uncomfortable by the invitation of Ralph to join the supper but the soup was so good he dismisses any thought of not having whatever else is offered. He had half expected Ralph to say a solemn grace before eating commenced but there was nothing of the kind. After all, in these days of excesses having a meal three times a day is no longer the big deal it was fifty years ago. Except of course in some homes.

Behind them Travis, wearing an apron was fulfilling the duties of chef with admirable composure. Beef burgers, made of pure beefsteak with all the trimmings followed. He says apologetically: "This has to be a makeshift meal but the next will be homemade and I hope will suit your gourmet tastes better." Ralph smiles. Raf remains as solemn as ever while Singer looks slightly puzzled but for once he manages to stifle his natural journalist curiosity and he holds back from probing into the background of the highly efficient chef.

Ralph says to Singer: "You and I have got to put our heads together but not now. We'll meet tomorrow when it suits you."

"Raf says he's quite happy sleeping in the gym and I have contacted my wife. She doesn't know the full story yet. She lives in our house in Kensington where she is the local church warden and very heavily involved in church matters, charities, and being a good Samaritan to all her friends. I fully approve of what she does."

"I also need to have a heart to heart with Raf but we'll take our time. Enough that we're here together to face whatever comes tomorrow."

Travis puts a plate of fresh fruit on the table. "That has to be the dessert for this evening. I can recommend the mangoes. I've become a bit of a specialist in mangoes lately."

With the eating done, Ralph and Singer help with the washing up while Raf retires briefly to the bathroom to clean himself of the mango juice which had run down his cheeks and chin.

All four look much more relaxed as they sit down on the comfortable chairs facing the chancel. Ralph and Singer sip their wines while Raf enjoys coca cola.

"Well Raf, I must confess, seeing you here this evening feels like a huge bonus, and a very nice surprise." Ralph could hear his voice tailing off as he looks into the light blue eyes of the boy.

"Jonnie says there will be problems?"

The two men look expectantly at Ralph. "Before we get on to those, do you mind if I ask why you decided to return?"

"It is what I want to do," he says pointedly, "I liked what you told me about Paul. He had two lives. When he walked on the road to Damascus God spoke to him and he became a new man. I would like to become new like that. Can you help me?"

Travis and Singer again look expectantly at Ralph. "Maybe," he says gently, "a lot will depend on you. The birth of Christianity was a wonderful event Raf – the greatest event in the history of the world. All religions have borrowed ideas, bits and pieces, and some chunks from certain events to create their own religion. Fanatics in your country and intellectuals in my country may decry Christianity but if they look closely they find traces of it in the way they live their lives today."

"It is all about God, and Jesus and his death on the Cross, and Paul. Forget about everything else. We are talking about history and what happened. Forget about religion and forget about what you think you know about Jesus. Don't worry about your stay here with me. You are very welcome. It will be as much a challenge for me as for you. And if you have problems don't be afraid to tell me about it. In this country you are allowed to change your mind if you don't like what I tell you about the All Powerful invisible God that we trust. I think that is enough for tonight. I suspect you have spent all day thinking about what you should do, and you must be tired. It is not possible to spend 24 hours a day trying to be close to God. It can't be done, and God does not expect that of you. He knows you are an earthling and with that comes a lot of responsibilities. To be a man you need to grow up normally, get a job and become part of your community. God is always there and you can make contact any time you want to, standing up, sitting down, kneeling – the choice is yours. And when you really feel close you'll know, whatever position you're in, that being in the presence of God is the greatest thing you can experience on this earth. But for now, perhaps you want to use the gym. Exercise is good for the brain and the body...." He looks challengingly at the other two to see if either wanted to argue the point.

Raf immediately gets to his feet. "I was just thinking like that."

Ralph smiles and the other two men watch with fascination as Raf starts pounding the heavy bag with relentless concentration.

"You seem to be on the same wavelength already with the boy," Singer says thoughtfully. "From what I know about Raf, that is amazing. He's not just an ordinary Muslim."

"He's a boy who misses his mother. He grieves for her almost all the time. I will try and persuade him of the best way to find her again – but not yet," Ralph says.

CHAPTER TEN

As Lilah approaches the end of the road, punctuated by fewer stalls, she increases her rhythmical stride and her legs move with smoother efficiency. A couple of the men walking past her, turn for a second look of appreciation. Meeting Yusuf again today has left her feeling a hollowness that is rapidly filling up with fear and revulsion and her right hand searches for a handkerchief in case she wanted to be sick.

All the old emotions are surging into her consciousness except this time it feels worse, because there is suddenly a deadly finality about everything.

A bus appears as she reaches a request stop and just in time her hand shoots up and the driver stops. It is only a few blocks away from her flat but she has lost her appetite for exercise and just wants to get home.

As she unlocks the door to her two-room flat and her blurry gaze levels on the inside, she half expects some unshaven brute to be waiting for her with ammunition for her empty belt. She knows the next one around her middle will never be removed again. She has been prepared for a long time for this and her lack of fear surprises her. It feels as though it has been replaced by a sense of relief. For a rash moment she just wants to get it done - even the tears welling in her eyes is about release more than dismay.

The time has finally come and it has brought a raw sense of reality such as she has never before experienced.

A new dress will require care and skill. She must not attract any unwarranted attention. And neither must Raf.

But where is Raf? What will she do if he has really disappeared? He's only a boy coming up to 13. She has always been so sure they are exactly on the same road she has never doubted he will be at her side when her time is up. For a moment it feels as though she may be becoming unhinged. What or who will be the target? Not that it matters, except the price is higher, the more important the individual is. She needs Raf. He has been her only prop on this journey even though he is such a small boy.

She watched him working for his father, carrying things and running everywhere delivering messages. There is such purity in what he is hoping to achieve. She is far less sure about herself. Where is all that inner strength she always believed she possesses? Will Allah give her a sign that all is well and that she is doing the right thing. Ever since the bomb, her life has stopped and she has been preparing for this – her revenge. Why should life be such an anti-climax? She feels shocked for a moment and looks behind her, half expecting to see Yusuf ready to reprimand her for having doubt. when the winning post is in sight.

This journalist Jon Singer, he must know where Raf is. He is writing a story. Raf will go down in folklore. She will merely be the barren woman who helped him. Encouraged she walks to the bed and searches among the change. This is an emergency call, and such calls must only be done on a public telephone. She grabs a bit a of paper and walks swiftly from the room, into the street and towards the red box forty yards away.

"Hello, is that Mr Jon Singer" her husky voice asks demandingly. Silence, then "Who is this?"

"I am the woman Raf has been staying with. What has happened to the boy? He cannot simply disappear like this. He is part of a family, a very special family, and I need to talk to him. The family do not know about you, yet, but if you don't help me to find him today the others will come to you and I think you should prefer to deal with me."

Singer feels dumb with shock by this explosive intrusion. Suddenly the menace he had felt briefly while driving Raf back from Canterbury was back tenfold.

"I will call again 20 minutes from now and then I must know where the boy is, or he must phone me."

She almost bangs the phone down, hesitates for a moment and then returns to her flat. That was the only way she wanted to handle it. This was not an occasion for polite negotiation. She was made fully aware of that the only time Yusuf has looked into her eyes to say the deadline has arrived. He emphasized the care with which everything had to be done, or else the remaining people afterwards would be paying the price. She knew she did not want to make a mess of it.

She repeated to herself that what she is doing has nothing to do with fear, or rage – it is all about justice, the justice of Allah. Their actions are calculated to produce maximum chaos, fear and lack of faith in the establishment. She did not bother to tell him that she understood. She knew he relied on her and she also knew that in fact revenge did not really come in to it. That was not her nature even though she knew that the thought of revenge had been the driving force while she was clinging to life. She always hated what had happened to her family. More than that she hated what had happened to her. Everything in her life suddenly changed and afterwards she often wondered why she was so desperate to stay alive? Allah did not help, and for the first time she wondered if he was a selfish God. All she asked for was a sign that it was all worthwhile. But there was nothing except the assurances from her Imam that it was not for her to expect divine intervention until she has earned it.

As she re-enters her flat, her first thoughts are about herself and the unclean feeling suffocating her emotion. Was it because she found this man bringing her a mango once every fortnight attractive and was it because she thought he was looking at her as though she was a real woman with normal appetites, when her only enjoyment now comes from eating a superb mango once every two weeks when she is given her allowance money for the flat and her food.

Her hands unbutton her top and her slacks and when the last bit of underwear drops to the floor she takes a deep breath to look at herself in the mirror. She always starts with the right side first; the unscathed side, and then she slowly turns until the full horror of the scars from the massive burns caused by the Israeli bomb are in full view. Every time she is unable to stem the revulsion she feels as she stares at her ravaged, twisted and multicoloured skin and she is never able to look for long. Only one man had ever seen her like this. His eyes had been full of desire, and passion and it was the first and only time she had felt the same and wanted to offer herself to him, but the shock in his eyes when he saw what she had warned him about, immediately ended what would have been her only afternoon of love. Poor Rudi just shook his head in disbelief and mumbled his apology like a child that he was sorry, so sorry and walked backwards from the room.

She had felt so crushed and humiliated. It was a moment of truth far more severe than she had felt when she lost most of her family in the explosion. She simply vowed she would never offer herself again to any man.

Lilah quickly walks into the bathroom and turns on the tap. Ten minutes later she breathes deeply as she again looks at her image in the mirror. A couple of years back she thought Allah might use the bath to restore her skin. But now she knows that is never going to happen. Even so she still cannot stop herself from taking a second look in case the bath had somehow managed to wash parts of it away.

CHAPTER ELEVEN

Suddenly her mobile lets out a shriek and she is startled, but then grabs it and immediately almost shouts "Raf, Raf, it must be you?"

The voice at the other end says softly: "Yes it is me."

"Where are you," she demands anxiously.

"I'm safe. I'm all right. Do you have any news?"

"Yes yes, I have news, brought to me today by himself, Yusuf. I've been all over the place in my mind, trying to think of where to look for you. It's been a nightmare Raf. I thought I had lost you. It was worse than that night when I had to walk home all the way from Hampstead and it took me over four hours. Everyone else is scattered all over the place, but I saw Yusuf today. Allah be praised you have phoned me. I spoke to Jonny Singer a short while ago."

He sounds unperturbed: "Yes I know. He phoned me."

"We need to talk Raf, but you know the rules. Not on the phone. Things are happening. What have you been doing and where are you staying?"

Silence then Raf says evenly. "I have met some friend of Jonny Singer and I was introduced to Paul."

"Paul? Who is he? What does he do?"

"Not very much. He's dead and he is now with God."

"What! You mean Allah."

"No, God."

"Oh Raf, I warned you not to get mixed up with these crazy confused Christians. What has Paul got to do with what we have to do? Just look at this leader they've got, he's like a chameleon, all colours, and all over the place trying to be everything to everybody, even us. He's off his head, because you and I know Allah needs martyrs. The Americans must be punished and we are starting to do it here in London. Our deadline will be very big."

After taking a quick deep breath she continues: "The people here worship everything, starting with themselves, then drink, drugs and sex. We are the honourable people with a just cause, and Allah is helping us and will reward the martyrs. But I must not say too much. We have to meet and talk today. I have been told to be ready. I need to buy a new dress and you need a new blazer and proper trousers. You can buy the best and most expensive clothes you want. We will look the part Raf. We will do it together. I was told today someone very high up is on a private visit somewhere. We must start the final phase tomorrow. You and I. Where are you?"

"I can't say."

"What? What is wrong with you?"

"Nothing. I also want to talk to you and I want you to meet someone and he will talk to you and then you and I will talk."

Lilah holds her breath. "And then what? Who is this man?"

"His name is Ralph, like mine but with an L in it."

"I thought you mentioned Paul?"

"Paul is with God. Ralph is here with me."

"And what about Jesus? What has happened to him?"

"Nothing. He's somewhere. Paradise is a very big place. He's with Paul I think. They talk a lot. Ralph owns his own church, and he has a gym inside. It's brilliant."

Lilah feels disturbed at the new tone in Raf's voice as he continues: "Paul is like the Muslims. He changed his name to become a Christian. Lots of people change their names when they become Muslims."

When he stops the huskiness returns to Lilah's voice as she says softly: "Do you think you're telling me something I don't know? Don't you want to meet your mother again and live with her in her palace in paradise?"

His response is quick. "Of course, but I think maybe it will be different. Ralph promised to tell me all about it and I want you to listen with me. You will like what he says. We have been together for so long and I want it to stay like that. Ralph is not about war. He uses different words and I want you to listen. If you don't like what he says I will leave with you. We are together Lilah and we must stay together. I trust you. That is what I want and I will phone you again soon."

Chapter Twelve

Travis stops as he reaches the turning into Copsem Gardens. From this vantage point it looks like a short cul-de-sac but it isn't. At the far end the road narrows and disappears from view between imposing rows of five-story houses. The church is situated parallel to the road with its front door facing a lawned garden and lychgate.

His mother now calls it the Old Church House. Before that she still called it St Paul's the Junior even though it was unused for about ten years before Ralph had bought it. Very few people remember it used to be called St Paul's. Was that why Ralph bought it? It would make sense. She always claimed it was the fact that the Church got greedy and sold the rectory to property developers. How could it possibly have survived without its own vicar? What sort of relationship could the regulars have with a dozen different clergymen sharing responsibility for their group of regulars?

Now it's almost as though the building has no proper identity, and when he brought this up with Ralph he did not seem bothered in the least. All kinds of groups now use the facility because it is rare in this part of the world to have a meeting place. Local teachers even use the hall for sports training. A sort of specialist sports training, because Ralph stipulated he would not have kids screaming the place down not knowing what they were there for. And somehow he has managed to control this. At night it was the time for grown ups but again he vetted the groups before allowing them to use the premises.

"This is not a picnic place," he told Travis with a smile "I like the idea that it has no proper identity. That fits in with the times we live in. Worshippers of the great all-powerful invisible God are better off not being called anything. That makes sure politicians, social workers and simply people specialising in finding something wrong with groups who enjoy meeting to discuss subjects of their own choice, don't find anything they can say is politically incorrect about this address."

"This is definitely no longer a church because I don't have formal services. We do sometimes enjoy normal bread and wine but never attempt to imitate any kind of ceremony. It is not a school, because lessons aren't delivered. It is a private place where interesting things happen, and where very absorbing subjects are discussed. The fact that I usually do most of the talking is neither here nor there. If I thought anyone attending had something useful or interesting to say I will always offer them the opportunity."

"It is a gathering place but with no definitive identity. The groups of young people, who use it, do so under the supervision of an adult who keeps control. I am always around and I keep an eye on it. Whenever I have been asked to say a few things, that is exactly what I do, I say a few things. If those who come here call it a gathering place for Christians, I don't mind. But I don't have a name for what goes on. If I am asked to demonstrate how to use the equipment in the gym, I do that, because I myself use the gym. I enjoy talking about Paul because I like him. Paul personifies all the problems faced by every human being who wishes to worship the God of Jesus."

Travis slightly shakes his head. He knows he is not on the same wavelength as Ralph and he wonders if he'll ever rise to that level. There is no doubt in his mind that it's his own fault. He has not been able to appreciate why Ralph refers to Jesus as plain Jesus, and Paul as the Pharisee who discovered the meaning of life on the road to Damascus.

While he was busy renovating the basement he heard a couple of young men referring to the address as simply Copsem Gardens, and that sounded right at the time. But of course, there is lot more to this plot of land. It feels like somewhere special and because of that he has become aware it must have a real history of its own. His mother was right. And Ralph has always said he gets good vibes whenever he walks into the place after having been away, even for a short time.

His relationship with Ralph has always been very solid. It was almost as though the basement job was created for him. No sooner had he confided in Ralph that he was interested in renovating buildings, in order to try and establish a second career for himself following his retirement from the security forces, when the call came from Ralph and the offer of the job. Not only that. Ralph had had three builders in for quotes, made up his mind what he was prepared to pay, and then offered the job to Travis.

And now, here he was back again, and he was half anticipating some sort of new offer – but what? Perhaps the plumbing wasn't working properly?

He has had three other smaller developing jobs in the area, but the competition is tough, well organised and established and that is why he now helps out on an infrequent basis with his friend's stall in the market. Fortunately he does not need to work. His retirement money, and the payment from the basement job, is well invested, and he knows, the way he lives, he needs never to work again.

His knee is playing up again today. Damp weather always seems to have this effect, but he has got used to it and has learnt to live with it.

As he enters through the lychgate a group of young people of both sexes, as well as a grown up, emerge chatting enthusiastically. He smiles and nods approvingly as he walks past them to the front door.

Whatever Ralph is trying to achieve, it looks as though he is doing just that. But he must, at least, be a bit eccentric not to charge rent for those who use the facilities. He is not surprised when Ralph opens the front door even before he has rung the bell.

"Thanks for coming so quickly," he hears him saying as he enters and then sees the slip of a boy pounding the heavy bag. Jon Singer, standing nearby, watches intently. Travis immediately recognises him. His curiosity is immediately stimulated as he stops and Ralph says: "Your mother informs me you're an all-rounder and I always believe what she tells me."

Travis faces him squarely and Ralph continues: "I know you cook all the meals in your house and have done for a very long time. And your mother tells me she did not even explain in the early days how you should boil an egg. The last time I saw her she said you've even started offering her French dishes and she wonders who on earth was teaching you. You don't have to answer that. The reason you're here is that I can see a situation developing for a chef and I thought I'd offer you first refusal – to fit in with your other duties at home."

Travis smiles broadly and shakes his head as he watches, intrigued, as Raf maintains a relentless, ferocious attack on the heavy bag. Singer walks to him and they shake hands.

"I'm afraid I have to be on my way as I've got a job to do," Singer says turning to Ralph: "But I will be back later on if I may."

Singer leaves and Ralph sees him to the door while Travis moves closer to Raf who is still giving vent to his feelings on the punch bag.

Chapter Thirteen

When Ralph returns Travis immediately lowers his voice: "What an amazing young talent. Is he from one of the local schools?"

Ralph shakes his head: "Take a seat. He's intending to have a stint on the treadmill afterwards."

Travis concentrates his attention on the older man. It is rare for the two of them to find themselves in a one to one situation to talk about matters unrelating to work, although he has been a guest at two of the talks that Ralph has given to younger people on the life of Paul. And from the business discussions they have had, he knows Ralph does his homework and then speaks directly and to the point.

"Raf is the reason you are here now." Ralph says, "He was invited by me to stay in this country to see if living the life of a normal boy would have the sort of influence on him, that I hope it will. I did not think at the time that there was any chance he would accept, because there are so many things about Raf's background and character that I am totally unfamiliar with."

Travis waits expectantly.

Ralph continues: "That was yesterday. Today on his way to Dover he changed his mind, and here he is doing something he loves doing."

"The problem is not with me, nor with Raf. He has made no demands or conditions. The problem is the political climate in this country and the way that British life has changed, and may continue to change."

"A boy like him cannot simply move in with a man my age, even if only for a holiday period of say, a month or two. He could be snatched away by anyone of a number of government institutions. It could also jeopardize my project here and the new life I am establishing gradually for myself. I need advice. You may not think you're the right person, but all the 'right' people that the authorities may recommend I would personally probably find unacceptable."

Travis intervenes. "Won't your wife help?"

"My project is also her project. She has remained living in our house in Kensington where she is Church Warden and very involved with various charitable organisations. She also baby-sits for a couple of our children to enable the wives to continue to work. It would not be fair to land this sort of problem on her. We meet once a week and so far that is working well but there is no telling whether this style of life will suit us. We have an agreement if one of us wants to return to normal married life the other one will agree. I decided this morning to talk to someone and you have drawn the short straw."

Travis sounds relieved. "I feel honoured sir, and delighted my cooking is not the real reason you wanted to see me. I agree you need a chaperone or even a few and I believe I have some of the qualifications you require." He stops as he sees Ralph frowning and he knows there is more to come.

"That is part of it. Raf is also an illegal visitor to the UK. He was smuggled into the country with his father." He pauses and frowns while searching for the right words to spell it out to the younger man.

Then the bombshell!

"His father was one of the two men shot by your former colleagues the other night in North London."

Travis almost jumps to his feet and stumbles away. As he regains his balance his eyes flash to the boy whose busy feet are still pounding the treadmill. When he turns to face Ralph again the worry lines show on his forehead.

"My first reaction sir, is that I am now an ordinary citizen. As such I have the freedom to be able to say to you that I recognise you are speaking to me in a very private and confidential capacity, and I want to assure you that no one will ever hear from me on this subject. I accept what you say so far, and if there is more to come I will treat every word with the same confidentiality."

"Thank you," is the immediate response. "Please take a seat. There are more details."

As he pauses again, Travis asks: "Do you know who helped with the smuggling from this end."

He nods. "You met him a few minutes ago, Jon Singer, the journalist."

Travis is stunned into further silence. Ralph continues: "It was a plan for a story – a scoop of the year perhaps – that went badly wrong. He thought he was helping father and son to escape to a better life, but they were using him to get into this country for their own agenda. A rather nasty agenda."

"The reason Singer was back here this morning, was to say he had heard from the woman where Raf has stayed since his arrival, but with whom he has lost contact, since the shooting. She instructed Singer to get Raf to phone her or else the remaining six more mature men she referred to as part of the family, would pay him a visit. Of course, he did not tell Raf that, and neither did I. The boy obliged by not telling her where he is currently staying. He has promised to phone her again and she is waiting for this to happen right now. I told Raf I need to discuss this with you."

"I have not reported this to the right authorities because I like the boy, and it seems he gets on with me. He's already sat through a couple of sessions of me talking about Paul. I suspect he really does have an interest, and if so, it probably means he feels very confused about religion and the belief that he has been promised a place in paradise with his mum. Perhaps he now feels that this promise is under threat and he wants to hear what I have to say on the matter. I have complete confidence in what I might say to him on this subject but I know I am up against the indoctrination he has been under all his life in Palestine. The wrong sort of interruptions from this woman and her six brothers, or whatever they are, could push the boy over the edge and it could take all of us with him. I need someone with your experience to ensure I don't do anything to precipitate such a disaster. If you feel unable to become part of such a venture, then you must speak up."

"I want to help Raf but I need to take it step by step. I do not want to try and convert him to become a Christian and I will simply not use the word. I do want to tell him about the All-Powerful and Creative God who loves his creations and who loves being in contact with his people.

I also want to explain to him who Jesus really is, and how Paul fits into the scheme of things. I do not call that Christianity – I simply call it a different way of approaching God, thinking differently, and doing things differently. I won't object if he ends up calling what I have told him, Christianity, providing he understands I am simply teaching him a different approach to understand and accept the story of Jesus."

The pounding suddenly stops and Raf gets off the treadmill, reaches for his lumber jacket he had hung over the chair and slowly shuffles towards the two men. Sweat is running freely down his cheeks.

"You know where the shower and bathroom is Raf. Help yourself and use the towel hanging next to the bath. By the way, Travis is moving in with us. He likes to mess about in the kitchen and is quite creative with the sort of meals he prepares. If you have any favourite food, or if there is anything you can't or won't eat then he is the man to tell. Providing it isn't some obscure Palestinian dish which only you know how to prepare, and in that case, you will have to instruct him how to do it."

The boy's eyes lower to the floor and it feels like minutes before he replies. "I have yet to find something I don't wish to eat. My father would have beaten me if ever I had refused the food my mother prepared and I would never have dishonoured her in such a way. I would like to watch you sometimes if that is all right? After my mother had gone to Allah my father and I mostly ate food that did not need cooking, or we had Palestinian veggieburgers."

"You'll be welcome Raf," Travis says.

Ralph rises. "About this friend of yours, the lady you spoke to a short while ago. How keen is she to meet with you again? How well do you know her?"

"Since my mother died, she has been my best friend, often cooking me a meal when my father was away," Raf says, "She is also a member of Hamas, and she received special treatment. Then when I joined Hamas at the age of ten, we were both looked after."

Ralph decides to risk probing deeper "Is she in any sort of trouble?"

The expression on the boys face remains unchanged as he lowers his voice: "I don't know because I have not seen her or spoken to her for two days. She is not allowed to have long telephone conversations. I only use my mobile to phone my father and her."

"How would she react if we invited her to come here to see you?" Both men hold their breath as they wait for an answer.

"I don't know what she'll say. Things have happened and she sounded unhappy. But she is an important person in this group she works with. She has this place where she lives and she has to look after it. If she comes to see me here the others might then come and look for us both. I have told her I have important news to tell her but I am not sure I want them to know where I am. I trust Lilah but things have happened. If I could talk to her I would know if I can still trust her. Do you want me to phone her and ask her?"

Ralph sounds reassured: "I like what you tell me about Lilah and as you can see, I have a lot of space. If she wanted to come and stay here with you, she would we welcome. But I hear what you say. If you're not sure you can trust her six friends then you must not let her know where you are. Let's think about it first. Go and enjoy yourself in the bathroom and try to relax. Do you have any spare clothes?"

Raf nods and walks away. "I have a shirt and trousers which we bought on the way to Dover."

"Perhaps you could ask Lilah to bring what you left behind, but that of course will tell her what your plans are." Raf frowns as he walks away. When he disappears Ralph turns back to Travis. "Why don't you walk to the gym and inspect the bit that Raf has left hanging on the chair. It first appeared yesterday and when he left it behind this morning and departed with Jon Singer I saw that as a beacon of hope. It is still hanging there, almost challenging me to either remove it, or to bring up the unmentionable subject with him. You'll know what I mean?"

He watches as Travis hobbles away and he holds his breath as the former MI5 specialist carefully examines the belt hanging over the chair. After replacing it he slowly walks back to reclaim his seat.

"I think there was a time when the belt was fully loaded. Equally I have no doubt you have made an extraordinary contact with this boy. And his conversation with the woman who wanted to make contact seems to underline that. I'm assuming you aren't aware of any further phone calls."

Ralph shakes his head. "There hasn't been time and he hasn't been alone."

Travis continues: "If she's looking for him it means they need him and want him. I can see nothing wrong with anything you have told me so far. But he does not strike me as a boy who is on the brink of throwing his own life away. If my reading of him is wrong, then it surely simply underlines the most horrific of threats challenging the western way of life. These people are among us, and they look like anyone of us and they act as though they are normal."

"I am honoured you want to draw me into this and my most immediate reaction to what I now know is that you hold the key to making an extraordinary breakthrough to the apprehension of this group of suspected terrorists. I know exactly whom to speak to and possibly what to do, but I will let you make up your own mind, because I know a bit more of you now, and I would not go against you. But I do pray to this great God that you speak of, that we must move quickly because I fear another monstrous atrocity is well on the way to strike at London again."

Chapter Fourteen

Travis, wearing an apron, is in full flow in the kitchen with a sizzling noise coming from a frying pan. Raf is sitting on a chair, his eyes following every movement. Ralph enters, also wearing an apron and says: "I might as well learn from the expert, and just wearing this thing makes me feel as though I'm making progress."

He looks closely at the sausages frazzling about from the heat, and continues, "... and just in case one or two of those decide to jump out, it is much better to be wearing the right outfit."

Turning to Travis he continues "I'm delighted to hear your mother's sister has offered to move in while you join us here for a period."

"It's a nice bit of coincidence, her offering this week to do just that in case I wanted a short break," Travis replies. "I shouldn't mind telling you sir, this is the best sort of break I could have wished for."

Ralph doesn't reply. He knows this highly thought-of former security expert knows all the right people at his former work place. Now if only they can somehow persuade Lilah to move in as well that will prove a tremendous boost to his efforts to get Raf to adjust to a new life. But he is under no illusion about the difficulty in persuading a mature woman to change her political and religious direction.

"Great, Travis. I'll leave it to you to make your own arrangements." Then he adds thoughtfully: "I bet your mother will disagree with you about coincidence having had an influence. She may see someone else deserving the credit."

Travis smiles: "While I was working on the basement I wondered who would be the first individual to spend a night there. I'd never have thought...."

Ralph interrupts "You're right. You will be one of the first. You'd better brace yourself. Jon Singer also seems to plan to move in for a time. I think he's worried that he's been under terrorist surveillance ever since he brought Raf and his father to this country. The call from Lilah today convinced him his days might be numbered. He thinks they may think he was to blame for the shoot-out in North London, regardless of the fact that he knew no more about it than I did. Just how do you persuade a modern terrorist they've got the wrong end of the stick? There appears to be no solution to mindless killing. I believe Singer when he says he thought he was on to a genuine scoop. It would be very ironic if it turns out to be the greatest news story he was never able to write. He would after all have to explain his own involvement. But I suppose that is what spin is all about."

Raf gives no indication that he might be listening to what was being said. He was trying to think of a way to bring Lilah to this address without her being aware where she is. She might regard it as making a clear break from Hamas, and Raf has no idea how she will respond to such a challenge. It would require a lot of courage, which he knows she has. But Hamas seem to have people everywhere and they do not allow anyone to give up membership.

He knows if she lost contact with them that the others would hunt them down. This is something they have never discussed or even thought of. There has never been an alternative to their plans to become martyrs for Allah. And if she comes, how will they tell Hamas that they have changed their minds and want a new life. Will Hamas allow them? What happens if Lilah does not like the sound of Paul, the man who made Jesus the Christ and the Messiah? How could she not respect such a man?

His thoughts are interrupted by Ralph saying to Travis: "If you really can't face spending your night time with a man who is so professional he could even interview you in his sleep, especially if he discovers your background, then you can take one of the rooms on the ground floor."

Travis looks sharply at him: "Can I delay my response to that one sir. And yes, I would prefer him not to know about ……. well, you know what. There was a lot of publicity at the time."

He pauses before continuing. "What is wrong with life in the Western World today sir and what can we do about it? How long do you think this new kind of terrorism will go on for? What would Paul have thought about it?"

His question surprises the older man who waits before deciding to accept the question at face value. "Curiously, Paul never mentioned wars or how to cope with them."

"When he launched forth to spread the word of man's new covenant with the Creator and his crucified son, he in reality declared war on ignorance, poverty of the mind, self-destructive life styles, and intellectual philosophies that were meaningless except that they seemed to be a provocative contradiction to the nature of God, and a challenge to His grace and righteousness."

"He would have been adamant in proclaiming that there is only one perfection in existence and that is to be drawn into God's presence in this life, either during it or at the end of it. He would have made it abundantly clear to any individual, that should they ever give themselves the right to challenge God about the rights they deem to be theirs to do whatever pleases them, they would simply have slammed the doors to His Kingdom in their own faces."

"He would have been highly critical of any authority or government if their laws appeared to encourage the young and the old to indulge in excesses of any sort, ignoring the stark facts that such a culture causes loss of self-respect, destroys character and personality, and degrades the spirit and soul of individuals. Life is simply so much more sophisticated now but I know Paul would have thought that too many people are totally uneducated in Christian life and that they were heading for a very painful death. And I am sure he would have urged the western world to sort out its own problems and values before trying to tackle the rest of the world."

Ralph looks closely at him "You're on the right track Travis. The old devil seems to have taken a leaf from the greatest spin-doctors of our time. No longer is he the nasty one with the horns and the fork and looking as though he has been dead for millenniums. Satan has been banished. Instead we now have Mr Sophistication with a face that requires hours of make up every day – the face of reason, albeit it a much distorted and twisted reason – that is helped by spin to sound uncomplicated, straightforward and transparent, but which is in reality without a spirit or a soul having the common sense to opt for the long time presence of our Father."

"These days you cannot condemn anything that makes logical sense to our minds. That would be to denounce the very foundations of the new society brought in by scientific political re-invention."

"The church cannot, won't be allowed to, and must not raise its voice in protest because that would be considered ignorant, narrow, bigoted, paranoid and deluded. They haven't a clue about the delicate balance between life in the flesh and life in the spirit and the supporting towers of faith. It's as though the middle classes have thrown in the towel and jumped on the bandwagon of excess. They are captivated by the new religion shrouded by a cloak of intellectualism. It is like a cancer of the mind finding its forgiveness and relief in the miracles of modern science, and the extremes we are fed as entertainment on our television screens."

"And if all this junk is repeated often enough it eventually deifies itself and is offered as the new sanctifying and forgiving goodness."

"In other words Travis, the greatest abuse that is taking place everywhere, and not just in the advanced societies of the world but also in the up and coming communities of the third and fourth worlds, where they are still learning to say please and thank you, is the destruction of the meaning of words that used to explain the power, the majesty and the eternity of Paul's experience on the road to Damascus."

"Celebrity without talent now has a power and omnipotence that the broadsheets and tabloids find irresistible. It sells because the readers keep buying."

"And the churches are failing to convince people that only God can strike into the hearts of man and remind him that he is accountable to a far greater power. The Bible is not without blame if you think how it describes what happened to Paul on the road to Damascus. Instead of explaining that Paul had been the recipient of the most wonderful experience any human being can have on this earth, it has left every Dick, Tom and Sally with the suggestion of a supernatural Jesus and a joke about a light at the end of a tunnel without providing even the slightest clue about the life-power emanating from the presence of God."

Ralph stops and looks at the other two. Travis had stopped preparing breakfast to listen and Raf is sitting rigidly upright on the stool.

His cheeks bulge as he breathes out. "I find it exhausting wearing my preacher's cap especially when I'm with two individuals in whom I have the utmost confidence."

His eyes rest on the boy as he says softly: "I hope you don't think I'm going to be talking like this every day from now on Raf – we're all having to think at speed – especially you. If it is a straight choice between religions then I am confident I can help you. If you're looking to escape from men who want to use you and Lilah for their own selfish, nasty and incomprehensible deeds then I know I can help you. If you seriously want to inherit paradise I feel just as confident I can put you on the right track. Life in the west is no picnic. Every day men and women face challenges in their lives, and success alone is not good enough. They are left exhausted and unable to set aside time to contemplate a life in the spirit which will automatically provide them with a much greater freedom than they are able to imagine. You're arriving at the right age because you're not even a teenager yet and I will make sure you enjoy the life of one. We will all help you. Right now talking is all I can do."

"And soon Jonny Singer will join us as well. He may not fit the pattern yet, but he keeps coming back, for whatever reason. He seems to think he may be safe here in this building and that shows he has come some way already." A smile touches his lips.

Raf jumps from the chair saying. "I think I will phone Lilah. I will tell her we have our own chef and that she will be free again to leave immediately if she does not like it here. If you have a car, I could arrange to meet her, in front of the tube station, and perhaps she will let me put something over her eyes so that she will not know where we are taking her."

Ralph chuckles. "In this country that is called kidnapping, and if Lilah reported us to the police we might get locked up for a long time."

Raf sounds puzzled: "I don't think so… (a slight pause)… sir. Lilah is not like that. I can't tell you about her, but I trust her. I trusted her two days ago and because I haven't seen her since I still trust her. But I know she met with the top man today and that only happens when there is news. She can't be happy because I am not with her anymore. We are a team. I am sure she was given news today. Perhaps she is unhappy enough to want to risk coming here to see me. I have a lot I want to tell her and I know she will listen."

There is a pause before Travis asks "And how can we be sure if we arrange to pick her up by car that she won't tell the top man, and we will drive straight into a an ambush."

Another pause, this time a bit longer as Raf struggles to find an answer. Then for the first time his eyes flicker as he says: "If Lilah has been given her orders, and the orders are for tomorrow or the next day then she won't come and there is no point in trying to get her here. But she did say one thing. She said we have to buy clothes and we have to visit the place where we have been told to be, to make sure we know it well and know exactly on the right day at the right time what we must do. If there is some spare time, then maybe I can persuade her to come. If Jonny Singer is going to be here, then maybe she would like to meet with him. I am sure no one blames Jonny. I was full of praise for him, and the others thought that he must have some sympathy for asylum seekers if he, a famous journalist is prepared to risk losing his career and freedom by helping to smuggle my father and myself through Calais."

The two men look at one another.

Travis says: "Go and phone her but see if she will say anything about the time factor. Ask her if she is seeing the top man again. Mention being picked up by car if you think she is interested and if she can be persuaded she is safe and even more important, that she will be safe from her friends suddenly calling on us. Tell her if she needs time and a place to think, this is such a place."

Raf starts leaving the room and stops when Ralph asks: "Would you prefer to use my telephone?" Raf shakes his head. "I like mine. It is the only thing that belongs to me." He stops as he remembers something.

The two men look tense as they look at the expressionless face of Raf: "When I met Jonny here at this church for the first time I had to tell Lilah where I was going, and I remember explaining to her how Jonny told me where to go. She did not try to stop me then, perhaps because I told her Jonny was going to give me some money, for something I had done for him."

The two older men look meaningfully at one another. Travis whispers: "So she knows where you are."

The rasping sound of the front door bell startles all three.

Chapter Fifteen

Travis immediately offers to see who it is but Ralph holds his arm and walks past him and Raf. His purposeful strides slows a bit as he approaches the front door and when he reaches it, he stops to brace himself, shuts his eyes for two seconds and then opens it. Travis pulls Raf back into the kitchen. They listen. Raf immediately recognises the voice and says: "It is Jonny."

At the front door the two men look straight at one another for a lingering moment. Singer, as though having read Ralph's mind, says slowly: "As far as I know I am alone. I purposefully took a long way around and paused several times to make sure no one is following me. I have some blankets in the car," He pauses then adds apologetically. "It is extremely nice of you to offer me … (pause) refuge. This feels like the safest place to be."

"Leave the blankets until we know if we need them. Come in. We're in the process of having supper, and you're welcome to join in," Ralph says briskly and beckons Singer to follow him.

Raf emerges in the doorway and announces: "We have a chef, and I like his food. It is different."

Travis chuckles and shakes hands with Singer. Ralph enters the kitchen with a bottle of wine.

"Never let it be said that any occasion can't be turned into the right occasion for a glass of wine. There is some coke in the fridge Raf." The boy immediately walks towards it and carefully opens the door.

Singer sounds troubled. "It's as though this whole business is taking off on a life of its own."

"Only if we attempt to resolve all the problems on our own sir," Travis says evenly, "but I understand it is not as straightforward as that.

There is really no point in us fretting until we have to. Raf seems to be in touch with what is going on."

"I suggest he makes his phone call," Ralph says quickly, "and then we'll consider the result and see if we have any options." Singer looks anxiously at the two men. Raf edges towards the door, expecting to be told to wait. No one says a word as they watch him leaving the kitchen.

"He's going to speak to the woman who called you earlier to see if she is prepared to join us." Ralph says.

Singer sounds nervous "With all due respect, is there any point in letting them know where we are?"

All contemplate what he has said and then turn to look at Raf who says on his return to the kitchen: "There is no answer .She keeps her mobile switched off while she is travelling."

Ralph is unable to disguise the much more concerned tone of his voice "Come in Raf, and tell us what you know, or what you're prepared to tell us. If you have decided to make your life here with us, you have become one of us. If things were normal we'd just let you slide in slowly to find your new feet and to decide in your own time if this is really what you want."

"But things are not normal. Not for us. We understand you are a very courageous boy from a very difficult young life and you've arrived here with us in rather extraordinary circumstances. I like you and I am prepared to trust you. The way I serve my God, is to be prepared to take risks. In the times we live I believe we must all sometimes take extraordinary risks. None of us here know what is happening. You may know some of what is going on. I have not tried to persuade you to tell us. Travis hasn't either. Travis is my friend, I trust him. I want you to trust Travis. He is not here simply to cook our meals. He is like you, a man of great experience, and his work has been to protect the British people against strangers who wish to use the freedoms we enjoy in this country, to unleash the forces of hell and destruction on innocent people. I know you also suffer in Palestine, but you and I must not disagree, if that is possible? My God does not want martyrs and does not approve of people who want to destroy other people in the name of martyrdom. He is totally against it. He does not believe it helps or makes any difference except to cause much suffering and unhappiness and this interferes with his business. It only makes matters worse. Travis was shot six times, here in London by a trapped terrorist and he is now retired because of it. But he still knows the people who are there to protect people like us from such events. These people are called MI5 and one call from Travis and they will surround this place. Before you and I can really get on with our lives we must resolve this. On this occasion I owe it to the people who live in this country and on this occasion my God expects me to help stop this."

"I would like you and Lilah to join us. I have offered you a new life, and I will offer her the same, if I get the chance. Right now there are many men like Travis here who are looking for the friends of your late father. I am not asking you to betray your father. But if you think they know where you are and will come for you, then I want you to tell us, and if you then decide you want to leave this place I will let you. Travis won't stop me from letting you go. He has said so. You know you can trust Jonny, because you trusted him all the way from Palestine. He brought you here and he has given you work. You know he has not betrayed you in any way."

He takes a deep breath, "That is who we are. Who are you Raf?"

The boy stands motionless, his eyes looking past Ralph and the other two men.

His reply is flat and soft: "I have not betrayed you sir and I don't know if Lilah has. I trust her completely but things are now different. My father is dead and he has been replaced by Rachid to represent Palestinian freedom fighters in this country."

Travis shuffles his feet as he prepares to interrupt. "This Rachid, is he the sniper, the marksman, who is also an expert bomb maker?"

Raf nods "There are six of the group left and they all move about separately. There won't be a group together looking for me. Two are dead and three are in prison. There are others but I don't know who they are. If they knew I was here they would come for me, but I don't think Lilah will tell them. I heard in her voice things have changed, and she does not trust what is happening. She is angry too, because she was told by the top man that without me she is worth less than half what she was worth before. Her money is to go to her family but now she is not sure. I don't know what he said to her. Lilah and I are a team. She won't tell them where I am. And she is important. She looks after that house for the organisation. And the MP sometimes calls her."

"A British MP?" Travis asks, alert.

Raf nods. "I don't know who he is but he is the one who knows where politicians go on private visits. Lilah told me he wanted to visit her, and take her to a place where they serve the best food – not in London, but she refused. She's not very interested in food unless she is hungry. I think the MP thinks she will be in the UK for a long time. I don't know if he knows I have been smuggled in." Singer shuffles his feet uncomfortably but no one looks at him.

"I would like to accept your offer sir. I will do my best to become British. There is nothing left for me in Palestine. Lilah is all I have left. She has suffered very badly but together we are a team."

"I like the way you talk about God as your friend, and who forgives people and who makes no demands for things to be done, and also Paul – and I would like to know more about Jesus, because in school we are taught many different things about him. You say you can tell me who he really is and I want to know how he will help me to see my mother again. Lilah is like me. We know our religion is not the same for everyone and that confuses us. We are members of Hamas because we had no choice where we live. I will keep trying until Lilah answers her phone. We were trained to be very careful not to use it too much, or for too long because your police are very clever to find out where we are."

Chapter Sixteen

It is several hours later and Ralph checks that all the doors are locked. The stained glass windows are covered by long dark red velvet curtains, and through them the street lights cast a soft glow around the auditorium. He is just finishing lighting a dozen candles, placed in strategic places to add to the cosy warm ambience. Travis is clearing up in the kitchen helped by Raf while Singer is in the basement investigating the sleeping arrangements.

Lighting the candles is only done on special occasions and this is an addition thought up by Ralph's wife. He knows she would have approved lighting them on this occasion. He may never have three more significant individuals spending the night. Will it be a one off, or will it be for an indefinite period? He stops as he feels tension warning him that something is about to happen.

A sudden scraping noise outside the front door startles him and he immediately walks to the spy hole. At first there is nothing to be seen but then a woman's hand reaches for the doorbell. Her finger reaches forward for a swift apologetic stab and a short sharp ring has Travis and then Raf appearing from the kitchen. Moments later Singer arrives through the side door.

Ralph watches intently as a woman's face appears. He knows immediately that he has never seen her before. As she steps back and comes into full view he sees she is wearing a knee length dark coat and black slacks. Her olive skin is set against free hanging dark shoulder length hair. It is almost an hour before midnight. There is no sign of another person behind or next to her and she gives no indication that there might be one. Her dark eyes reflect expectancy as she looks up at the door.

His right hand lifts the bolt and opens the door a couple of inches.

"Who is there?"

Her reply is immediate and to the point.

"It is urgent for me to speak to Raf."

Silence. Ralph hesitates. She had sounded anxious but he feels very cautious.

"Who is with you?" he asks.

"No one. I am alone," is the immediate reply. "I took a bus into the West End and then I walked here to make sure I am alone."

He does not hesitate any further and opens the door to look closely at Lilah, who keeps her left hand remaining in a coat pocket. She says: "You are not the journalist, you must be Raf's new friend?"

He says: "I hope so. Come inside."

Her "thank you" is barely a whisper as she takes a couple of steps inside and then stops to look at the lit candles and the boy in the distance. Ralph looks closely at her but is unable to ascertain whether the coat is obscuring anything bulky around the top part of her body. His entire body quivers as he realises that even if there was something , that it would already be too late now to resist her in any way. She has not removed her left hand from the pocket. For a moment he wonders if he has made the most disastrous decision of his life, inviting her inside.

She turns to look into his eyes and says softly: "My name is Lilah. Raf has been staying with me."

He nods: "We were hoping you'd come. Raf has been trying to phone you."

She turns to look at the boy slowly walking towards her and says: "I am never switched on in public." Ralph feels impressed by the strength of discipline that clearly must exist within the entire group.

As Raf gets closer he stops, his face remaining expressionless. But his voice sounds slightly more relaxed "We were going to invite you."

"So I hear." she says. "I saw someone tried to phone me, and I knew it must be you. It is nice to know I was expected. I decided to come here because I did not know where the journalist lived." She shrugs her shoulders slightly. "I would have chosen this place anyway, because I know you and I knew this is where you would have preferred to come."

Ralph is quick to recognise the implication of what she has said. Already he knows they must have a special relationship but he is unable to shake off the strong feeling of unease. Religion clearly plays a massive role in their relationship but the fact that the boy's only ambition seems to be to join his mother in paradise is not entirely reassuring.

She turns to Ralph: "You must be the man of God? According to Raf?"

He hesitates, then: "I am a happily married man. I have three children and they are happily married and have children."

"Then you are indeed a man of God," she says softly. "I believe Raf."

He beckons her towards a seat "You must be exhausted and cold."

"A chair would be nice," she answers softly and her face lights up as she sees the large comfortable chairs. Travis has not yet emerged from the kitchen. He drew back in amazement when he recognised Lilah, the beautiful woman with a desire for a sweet ripe mango once every two weeks. For a moment he almost felt panic-stricken but then managed to control himself. Has she had supper? Is she hungry? There is some food left, and then his eyes light up as they fix on the one remaining mango - the one meant for himself. For some curious reason he had postponed enjoying it. Reality then strikes home and he chucks the drying up cloth on the table and walks purposefully swiftly from the kitchen, past the others and towards the front door. His right hand unbolts it and after a moment's hesitation he opens it and steps outside. There is no one to be seen in the walk to the lychgate. His knee warns him not to walk so swiftly and he slows down. There are no pedestrians to be seen anywhere. It really is a quiet road. And while there are a number of parking spots available there is no one to be seen sitting in a car.

"She must be alone," he murmurs to himself. "I wonder what has happened to the bearded bloke with the furry coat."

Once again he recalls the furtive handing over of what looked like a brown envelope and the strange manner of their walk down the street, going in the same direction but not together. This bearded man may be the top man? His heart starts pounding with excitement. He must have an immediate word with Ralph. His instinct tells him that this individual may be known to MI5. If so this whole business could be cleared up in days, and that could include arresting the MP.

Despite his knee objecting again he rushes back and bolts the door firmly, and then walks to the side door leading to the basement to make sure that it is firmly locked as well.

Lilah is talking to Raf and doesn't look at him as he walks past her. Ralph watches Travis closely and when he returns to the kitchen he walks after him saying: "She claims she has just walked all the way from Piccadilly to make sure no one was following her. And for some reason, I believe her." Then he stops abruptly. Travis is clearly very concerned and is about to tell him why.

Chapter Seventeen

Ralph waits patiently as his friend lowers his voice. "I know her," he whispers, "for the past couple of months she has been my favourite customer in the fruit market, and you just have to look at her to know why."

"Once every fortnight she would turn up and ask for one ripe mango, and I made sure she had the best. She always addressed me as though I might be the one having difficulty with my English, and I so looked forward to her appearances that I was always tongue tied when she asked the same question every time."

"She was there again today. But this time there was this bearded individual who gave her what looked like a small brown envelope. They barely spoke. Of course he may have been there on previous occasions but I don't recall ever spotting him before. It was a very strange meeting – short, secretive and not a sign that they wanted to talk to one another. But he must have had something to tell her, and come to think of it, they may have had a conversation while walking in the same direction. I did not watch all that closely because I had customers. He may have been the top man delivering her instructions. If she had gone to Piccadilly there might have been another reason for that. It may be that without Raf their plans have altered. We know these people will use one suicide bomber to eliminate another if they deem it necessary. We know that insiders can never leave Hamas. There is no second chance. This organisation is that deadly serious about their horrific work. And if they think we all know about them, she could be here on a mission."

Ralph feels the blood withdrawing from his cheeks as he says: "She looked pleased about the easy chair and relaxed into it. If she is under pressure she is remarkably cool about it. But I believe so many of these individuals are. Her hand has not left her pocket in all the time she has been here but it doesn't seem to me as though there are any bulky extras on her upper body. I even thought she must be in great shape if she walked from Piccadilly. But all that means nothing. Modern technology is so sophisticated. I thought her eyes softened when she looked at Raf but it feels hopeless to try and read what is going on. Raf never shows any emotion, but my instincts allowed me to let her inside. Even when Raf saw her appearing out of the blue he did not exactly give her a big welcome. Will he ever learn to smile again?"

Travis appears to be wracking his brain about something, and says: "I think the time has come for me to make that phone-call sir. There are always people on duty. Some of them only become alive at night."

"But would that really do any good Travis, or even save our lives? Even if by now this place was surrounded what good would that do? If Lilah's finger is on a button then all of us had better start preparing to meet our Maker. I'm going out there and I will take it as it comes. Raf said he wanted to invite her to come over and talk. They must have had some discussion about coming here. Unless they suspect we are a danger to them, and have already passed judgement on us, there seems to be very little we can do at this stage."

"I will offer her a drink and then you can join us. Let's see how she reacts when she recognises you. I won't mention religion. We must be cautious what we say. The ball is entirely in her court. She came here with a purpose, and we don't know what it is."

"Pity your God doesn't offer a special kind of bomb proof vest sir," Travis says laconically.

"Oh but he does, Travis" is the swift friendly response, "I just hope we have enough time to allow me to help you to discover how it works."

CHAPTER EIGHTEEN

As he walks back inside Ralph is just in time to hear Lilah say: "I take it your presence here means you are writing about Raf?"

Singer looks and sounds defensive as he stutters his reply: "Well not exactly Lilah. I am thinking about it but I haven't yet worked out a way to keep myself out of it. As you know I helped Raf and his father to enter the country against the normal rules, and now his father has disappeared."

She looks thoughtfully at him, and Ralph decides to rescue Singer. "You must be hungry and thirsty Lilah. Are you used to walking long distances?"

"Back home I walked everywhere. Raf will tell you. But I did have a sandwich at Green Park tube station."

"What about a glass of wine, or a hot drink, coffee or tea or chocolate." She shrugs, and looks boldly into his eyes: "Can I start with a hot chocolate?"

Ralph nods with a tight little smile and feels encouraged. That at least did not sound as though she was asking for her last drink. Perhaps she is doing exactly what they are – playing it by ear and preparing for every eventuality.

"And can I also have a hot chocolate please?" Raf chips in.

"Of course, and what about you Jon?"

The journalist again feels trapped. He would have immediately asked for a double or treble whisky, but even he knows this is not the right occasion.

"Chocolate sounds great thank you, but I think I'll opt for a glass of red wine, if it's on offer."

Ralph nods and walks away and disappears into the kitchen only to emerge again a couple of minutes later. He takes a seat on Lilah's left side, with her hand still in a pocket, saying: "Raf was very concerned earlier He thought he had lost touch with you."

Lilah moves her eyes from Raf to look evenly at Ralph. Then she says softly: "I know Raf well enough to appreciate there is a slight change in him. When we spoke earlier he used words I have not heard him use before. Now that I'm here I see it must be your influence. Raf says you are a man of God. This is a Christian church. Is it your church?"

"It is my home. I have invited Raf to stay here with me. I know he would like you to do the same."

He holds his breath and is immediately aware that she chooses not to reply to the invitation as she says: "You look like a man at peace with himself, and you have a very nice church. I love the curtains and the candles. It helps to make one feel relaxed. It is said men who are at peace with their God are at peace with themselves and those around them."

Their eyes are locked as he says softly: "Real peace only comes to those who can spend most of their days in the presence of God. In reality that can only happen when we move from this life into the next. We cannot escape the tasks we set ourselves every day. I wonder sometimes what God thinks about all those who spend most of their daily lives hiding away in huge institutions, without making contact at all with the real world and its problems, challenges and threats."

"Why are our worlds so different?"

"Well that is what Jesus was all about. He wanted to tell everybody that the Kingdom of God starts on this earth, and he wanted to teach people to think differently and to do things differently so that everyone could knock on the door of the Kingdom of God. And, again, if you think about it, what better way than to persuade everyone to pray to an all-powerful, loving and forgiving God on a daily basis? That shapes your mind, your character, your daily life, and your relationships. If your heart is full of love for your God then everyone around you will benefit."

He blinks as her voice resounds harshly: "But then Jesus was killed by his own people. Why did God allow that to happen? Was Jesus also a martyr? In our religion we believe in being martyrs."

He takes his time to reply: "We are not exactly sure who was responsible for his death, but it was most probably a conspiracy between the Romans and some Jewish intellectuals. And there is a huge difference. Jesus did not ever kill anybody nor did he ask his disciples to protect him when he was arrested. Even on the cross he had time to say to the man next to him, that he would be forgiven his sins, because it was clear he was a good man at heart. He promised him they would both be in paradise. Some people wait very long before they are prepared to reveal their true nature and character and declare their commitment to a love for fairness for their neighbour. God prefers for people not to die until they are ready. That is why it is wrong to take someone else's life. Being a mindless killer shows an arrogance, selfishness and vindictiveness that deeply offends God the Father. People like that will find it very difficult to recognise the light and power of God's presence."

Singer and Travis both anxiously watch the pocket of Lilah's coat so see if there is reaction. But her face remains expressionless as she looks ahead of her into the chancel.

Ralph breathes deeply but quietly and then says calmly: "Paul was the first man ever to experience the forgiveness of God after having been a nasty person who persecuted the Christians, before God showed him how wrong he was about Jesus."

"Before his conversion Paul wanted the followers of Jesus to be destroyed because he felt it threatened his own religious culture and life style. The Bible without the humanity of God is meaningless, and a nasty God without love is of no use to us. We are all given a free will and that is why God values our love, and why he wants us back with him. It sounds like a constant battle on both sides, and God is aware in this country there is a lot of disinformation being spread everywhere about himself. That is one of the curses of living in a free society like ours"

"Is this your own private church?"

"Yes it is, and it helps to explain why Christianity is having trouble today. Many churches have closed down. Our world is now so sophisticated many children are born into a life, and environment where they have no hope of surviving into balanced grown-ups and then they turn their anger against their culture, their values, and even against themselves and never manage to rise above this handicap. It is my home but I also have people who still use it as their place to sit quietly and think. They don't really want to talk to me or anyone."

"Where are your family?"

"We have a second home, and my wife works for another church. We meet once or twice a week, or we talk on the phone regularly."

"Why do Christians call Jesus God?" She asks suddenly. Ralph lowers his eyes and says: "I would rather not give you the full answer to that on this occasion. I would like you to join Raf and stay here with us. But for a start, I would ask you to watch and listen and to save your questions until you are sure you can't answer them for yourself. I will of course be available at all times should you wish to talk."

"But I will give you part of the answer to your question right now. The most important evidence, and good news about Jesus is that he was crucified so that we might live forever. Because of Paul we are absolutely certain that Jesus is alive and very well and living close to God. The true message of the Cross is as simple as that. Everything else you think you know about Jesus is almost irrelevant. The fact that the crucifixion did not kill Jesus is what it's all about. And just to make absolutely certain that the event was not forgotten as time passed, Paul was stopped on the road to Damascus, and introduced to the real live Jesus to show him that our God is a God of love and power and forgiveness. The evidence emanating from what happened on that fateful day at Golgotha proved nothing else. Jesus was Jesus and he suffered terribly so that the truth could really get to those blessed with the faith to accept that God, on that one occasion required drastic measures to get through to humanity that life on earth is not the hopeless, pointless exercise that the actions of so many mortals try to convince us it is."

At this moment Travis arrives carrying a tray with mugs of chocolate and a glass of red wine. Lilah stifles a gasp as she recognises him and rises to her feet in amazement, still keeping her hand firmly in the coat pocket.

"We meet again," Travis says warmly, "and this time it won't cost you anything. This is on the house."

Her lips part in a gentle smile as she reaches for a mug, and then turns to Ralph: "This gentleman sells the most delicious mangoes. I discovered him two months ago and saw him this morning when I went to the market."

There is not the slightest hint that she feels uncomfortable for having been reminded of the occasion. "Now I feel surrounded by friends. Raf's friends and mine."

She sits down and the others follow. Travis walks to the kitchen and returns immediately with a huge mango balanced on his fingertips. This time Lilah flashes a broad beautiful smile as she again rises to her feet. Raf watches closely.

"Two mangoes in one day," she exclaims. "Must I thank Allah for this, or was it Jesus? This is a house for Christians so I thank the Christian God. He will know this is very special for me. You must share it with me Raf. You didn't know about this weakness of mine. It is a very good sign and you are a very good man for the way you are spoiling me." Her voice drops: "Maybe it is my lucky day."

The smile fades as she retakes her seat and then looks expectantly at Ralph..

"I have always known there are differences between your God and Allah. Who can blame Raf for feeling influenced."

Travis feels his nervous tension rising again. Was that a challenge? Her left hands remains in the coat pocket. Ralph finishes his chocolate and rises to put the mug down on a small table in front of them. As he turns towards his seat he is surprised to see Travis sitting firmly in it.

"Excuse me sir," he says slightly uncomfortably "but I never thought I would ever have the opportunity to have a conversation with this lady. She comes and goes so quickly I feel I must talk fast before she disappears again."

The smile returns to Lilah's face before she says softly: "No one has ever called me a lady before. (pause) I am not in a hurry. I still have to talk to Raf – he is my best friend. We have been best friends for a long time."

Travis slowly breathes again.

"Are you with the church as well, even though you work in the market?" she asks.

This time Ralph intervenes: "Once a week only, when his friend goes to Covent Garden to get fresh produce. He is also a builder. He renovated my basement and built on extra bedrooms at the back. You should see it."

Lilah looks thoughtfully at Travis who says "What a nice coincidence –you and I both going to the market on one day a week and always choosing the same day, except that it was every two weeks for you."

Lilah allows herself a mysterious little smile as she recalls how carefully she had planned her visits to the market to try and ensure that he would be there – if only because the mango-ritual and the warm eyes of Travis was the only event of interest in her life the past number of weeks. Raf watches and listens intently. Even at his age he is able to appreciate the chemistry at work between Lilah and Travis. How will she react to this? Singer also watches closely, and he feels equally unsure whether Travis is pressing the right buttons.

Lilah returns to her unanswered question: "Now tell me – are Jesus and your God the same?"

Ralph has never seen Travis looking so tense. So far he has been unable to decide whether Lilah is simply very relaxed, or whether she is supremely confident about her own position.

"You know about Paul." Ralph asks and she nods.

"Paul is at the heart of what is called Christianity. In his own heart he was always an honest and humble man who grew to be arrogant when he lost track with the true nature of the God of Israel. Most of the New Testament in our Bible is about Paul, but so many crucial details were left out. No one knows why, but you must remember that all religions were created by people, and people are fallible. Some Jews claim the Torah was there before God created the earth, but I think that is wishful thinking, even though Judaism is the oldest One God religion. The creation of heaven and earth is God's great experiment. And if you consider that every individual is born with a powerful free will you can imagine the difficulties the Creator had. The next life is as invisible as He is to us. Paul had a very important glimpse of it, and it was so powerful he became the second most amazing man in the history of the world. It is right that religions should learn from each other. Unfortunately the world is becoming such a successful business enterprise that people in this part of the world in particular, now believe that they don't need God anymore. That was what it was like in the days of Jesus. Prophets were walking around with special religious deals for sale."

"There is no doubt Christianity was in trouble after the crucifixion. The followers of Jesus were distraught, devastated and afraid. They felt alone and threatened."

"Then Paul arrived, a former persecutor of the Christians – now suddenly the biggest Christian of them all and all because God had decided it was time to personally intervene in a most spectacular and dramatic fashion. Paul was drawn into his presence and introduced to the living Jesus in the next life."

"Today the Church misinterprets this experience. They are losing touch with how a spiritual Creator can have contact with a material world. They ignore that God can make contact because each individual already has a spiritual life in him. It is the biggest challenge of all, getting the balance right inside our own minds. There will be a time when we leave our bodies in order to advance into the next much more agreeable life. Paul was still very much alive, when God used his power to prove to him that Jesus had preached the truth. Paul was given an insight into the relationship between spiritual life in the presence of God and life on earth"

"His first reaction was to feel thoroughly confused, and he was unable for some time to focus properly on what had happened to him. He needed the reassurance of a man called Ananias, leader of a group of Christians in Damascus, to confirm to him that he had indeed met Jesus, and to baptise him. Then as reality engulfed him and his spirit got to grips with what had happened his gratitude to God knew no bounds and this stayed with him all the days of his life. His love for his Father grew in strength daily and constantly and he made Jesus the face of his new faith. He could never accept that he had been blessed in the same way as Jesus, because he did not want to think of himself as being an equal to Jesus. He knew what a monster he had been to the followers of Jesus after his crucifixion. For him Jesus had to be the Son of God. He knew Jesus was the inspiration that had brought him to the Damascus Road for that all-powerful manifestation-the greatest blessing that could ever happen to any living mortal."

"But all the old arrogance, and the Pharisee self-assurance and posturing was gone and in its place remained the very natural and humble man – with his very special message and evidence. No one can come face to face with such an experience and not be stripped of all the previous nasty, ridiculous, human veneers and pretences."

"Paul's entire attitude towards Jesus changed immediately and dramatically. For him Jesus was the perfect individual, someone he had been personally introduced to by God. He knew Jesus was with God, and he knew that was perfection. At first he must have felt it was undeserved but then he understood that God wanted him to tell all the nations of the world that they would all be welcome to enter into his world in the next life – even those who had done terrible things but who had genuinely seen the error of their ways in time. We are the gentiles, you and I, and Travis, and Jon, and Raf. In Biblical terms, that makes us special, because God knew all gentiles were having problems. The suffering of Jesus was for us."

"That is how Damascus changed him and took over his life. That humility never left him, and that is why the New Testament is mostly about Paul spreading the news about a new Covenant with God, a new beginning, in a new world where God rules personally and people know there is a way to avoid desolation in death. Paul never stopped talking and thanking God and now he was able to introduce Jesus as the Son of God, to whom he remained eternally grateful for having been instrumental to getting his sins forgiven. He even said in his preaching that Saul had died, and that Jesus had taken over his life as Paul. For him it was more than a miracle. He was able to claim he had seen, and felt and experienced the ultimate, and he now understood what the meaning of life was. And so he made it his life's work to personally tell as many people as he could and that the way to God was through Jesus. All the sermons, all his preachings, and all the letters he wrote to the communities where he had set up churches revolved around his Damascus Road experience – and meeting with Jesus face to face."

"Centuries before that Jewish religious mythology produced news of a great leader and ruler coming to the aid of the Jews who were dispersed over many different lands. He would be known as the Christ, and many thought he would arrive on a magnificent steed with an indestructible sword in his right hand and he would destroy all Israel's enemies. He would become the King of the Jews. Then in the time shortly before and during the life of Jesus, the Jewish prophets spoke about a Messiah, the number one representative of God on earth arriving to take Israel to the new world free of disasters, sin and poverty. No true Christian could deny that Jesus was the number one representative of God on earth. I am quite certain that both God and Jesus are happy with such a description of the man who was crucified."

"During the three years when Jesus preached and taught people about the new covenant with the God he also called father, many thought he was the Son of God. I don't think it was a big deal with God the Father – our Father as well as yours. The words of Jesus were so challenging, so new, so convincing, so unique and so informative about the All Powerful, forgiving and loving God, it challenged and disconcerted everyone who heard him speak. But it also attracted enemies."

"Later on Paul gladly added his voice that Jesus was the Messiah, Son of God, the Christ and much more. What is important above everything else is that Jesus spoke about continuous life in the presence of his Father. Paul's way to show his gratitude for God forgiving him his sins by introducing him to a real live Jesus, was to acknowledge that Jesus was part of the essence of God's nature, and that he was responsible for Paul's conversion on the Damascus road."

" Jesus was the first man who was known to have been drawn spiritually into the presence of God. Paul was the only man at that time to have been given proof by the Almighty that this was so."

"He went on to spend the rest of his life telling as many people as he could, that the Kingdom of God was as available to everyone as much as it was to Jesus. God is the creator of all things and he does not live in a temple or palace and he does not need man's sacrifices. But he does want all the races to be friends and to honour one another."

"Jesus taught about life and living – discovering the real joy of both until it was time to move to the next life where total fulfilment and perfection awaited them. People pray to Jesus and ask for help and courage and direction but he does not intervene personally in anything to do with life and death. That is God's prerogative. Jesus can inspire minds to think differently and to do things differently. That is his power."

A stillness envelopes the building as the candles create a shimmering incandescence turning all those sitting silently, into ghostly figures, like saints.

Lilah's voice is barely above a whisper but everyone clearly hears her asking: "And the miracles, what about the miracles? Were they all done by God?"

"They were certainly all gifts from God, even though most were never properly recorded or explained." Ralph adds quietly.

"And is it a gift that we are here listening to you – Raf and me, from a different life, a different world? Are we looking for a different God? With different values?"

Once again her eyes lock into those of Ralph who says softly: "The world of Jesus and Paul is one world for all the peoples on this planet looking for peace and the love of God."

At this moment Travis reaches out and places his right hand on to the hand of Lilah in the coat pocket. She turns slowly to look at him as he says: "Your hand must be frozen. You have kept it in that pocket all the time you have been here."

The others collectively hold their breath. Even Raf knows the question has a special significance. His eyes widen slightly as he watches and waits.

Lilah slowly lifts her right hand and places it on the hand of Travis saying: "Yes it is cold, but lift your hand and I will show you."

He does and she slowly produces her clenched left hand to reveal huge disfigurement from a massive burn. Travis is shocked. Tears well in the eyes of Lilah as she watches him lifting her hand and her fingers relax as he presses them against his lips, saying "We all have scars."

All hold their breath as she rises to her feet, gently withdrawing her hand from his. Tears flow down her cheeks as she turns to step away from him, her head held high. Then she slowly turns to look straight at Travis, who has also risen.

"Yes, everywhere there are people with scars, but how many are like this?"

She takes another step backwards and removes her coat. As it drops her hand releases a catch and her trousers drop as well. The jersey and shirt follow and she stands in her underwear revealing dark massive scars down the left side of her body, leg and arm.

But even more shocking than that is the brown leather belt strapped across her chest and shoulder. Her hand again releases a latch and it slides to the floor. A wire is connected to a little box tucked away in her pants. Tears flow silently and freely down her cheeks.

"This is who I am. In Palestine we said it was an English/American bomb, but there was no proof. The Jews were proud enough to claim it as their own. I should have died quickly that day but I refused to and I told Allah or whoever was up there listening that I was not ready to die. I know it was my determination not to die that saved me. The doctors told me so. There was no sign to tell me differently. I came to England because I was looking for a miracle but I discovered there would not be one. The British MP fixed me up with a hospital for examination. Modern medical science still has a lot to learn. I will carry this with me all my days."

"Now you know and now you must help and protect Raf and me. That is if you are still prepared to help us. We do not want nor do we expect much. I don't know where I am going now and neither does Raf. Like Paul we want new lives and like Paul we are prepared to change Gods. Raf and I want you to tell us more."

Then she looks challengingly and expectantly at Travis.

He says gruffly, with his wet cheeks glistening in the candlelight, "I would like to be included in that. I have just as much to learn as you and Raf. (pause) I have always kept my distance from too much perfection, especially in a woman. When I look at you I do not see any imperfections, just war wounds. I have my own scars, given to me by someone from Hamas living in this country. Six bullets. I have never known who he was and I have never wanted to look for him. Now you and Raf and I can work together for a new future."

"The three of us?" she asks breathlessly.

Looking straight into her eyes he says fearlessly "We can adopt him and then we can make sure he comes here every day to become the fittest boy in whatever school we send him to. That will solve the problem of his presence in this country."

"You and me? You are a brilliant man Travis," Lilah says through her tears. "From the first day your hand reached for a mango hidden away beneath your counter, I suspected you have a generous heart and a very good clear way of thinking. Even then I felt full of appreciation."

"And no one will need to know," Raf says suddenly. He looks questioningly at Jon Singer and Ralph adds: "Providing you can persuade someone this is not the greatest story he never wrote about. But where will you live? Where else but in the basement below. It is yours for as long as you need it."

A hushed silence befalls the small group before Ralph continues: "It's about time someone tested whether the plumbing functions as it should and if it doesn't then you will know whom to blame."

Lilah eases into a chair looking straight at Raf and Ralph continues quietly: "Before we go any further, I think I will give my wife a call and invite her to dinner tomorrow to meet her new extended family. I can just imagine her surprise and disappointment when she hears what she has missed so far. And I will also speak to a friend of mine who runs his own parish not far away. I think it important we get on with what needs to be done. In the meantime Travis could give some thought to that phone call he needs to make."

"And Lilah had better sleep in the room next to me. I shall be honoured to be your chaperone. We may as well start at the beginning, and see where it leads us."

Watched by the others Ralph walks to the belt discarded by Lilah and picks it up. He then looks at Raf who immediately moves swiftly into the gym where he removes his own leather belt from the chair and hands it to Ralph.

"I left it behind this morning."

Ralph nods. "I noticed but I wasn't sure whether perhaps you just forgot about it. Giving it to me now in this way, is so much more preferable."

Chapter Nineteen

The dark shadowy figure of a man moves cautiously through the narrow garden separating the church from the equally large four-storey building. He pauses when he reaches the front of the house, and takes his time to ensure there are no pedestrians on the way. Then he lifts himself with laboured care over the medium high garden wall, pauses again, as he checks both ends of the road before proceeding to walk slowly past the parked cars, making sure there is no one sitting inside with their eyes on the gate leading into the churchyard.

When Travis reaches the lychgate he pauses to look up and down the deserted streets. In the distance two cars drive in his direction as he starts the walk towards the front door of St Paul's the Junior.

As he enters Ralph is seen putting out the candles. Singer immediately walks towards him and Raf is seen sitting in an easy chair with his knees pulled up under his chin.

"I think you can relax," he says to Singer, "Everything is quiet and there is hardly any sign of life. Lilah has assured me that she has told no one that Raf met with you and Ralph at this church. Her former colleagues would have been very angry with her for allowing Raf to meet with a representative of the Christian Church."

Ralph joins the two of them as Travis continues: "There is no reason to fret about the possibility of them suddenly arriving at this building looking for Lilah and Raf. If you feel that uneasy about it, then this must be your only night staying here. You should also consider moving flat, stop having your photograph printed next to your articles, even change your job or name or both, or at least have all calls to you at your office vetted properly before taking them. You could even consider moving to another country."

"I will be in contact with MI5 but I need to talk first to a couple of friends. I do not want to see Lilah and Raf taken into custody. That would also implicate your role in their being here in the first place. For that reason I have decided to wait until tomorrow morning to make sure I talk to the right people."

The three men slowly walk back to where Raf sits. Lilah appears in a long white dressing gown, looking relaxed and smiling as she says: "I can't believe I am the first guest to wear this beautiful garment. I have never worn anything like it before."

"Please accept it as a gift from me," Ralph says evenly.

"You won't be able to return to your flat for your clothes."

"There are so few," she says softly. "I will not miss anything."

"Is it time for another hot drink? No one is ready yet to sleep," Travis says as he walks towards the kitchen.

"And I want to help. You must teach me English cooking."

She takes hold of his right arm and they disappear into the kitchen.

Ralph takes a seat next to Raf and looks closely at him. "It has been a very eventful day. You will have difficulty in sleeping."

"I have had many nights like this. I can sleep, but I don't want to. Lilah looks happy and that is brilliant. I have never seen her looking so relaxed sir. I was very worried about her because I did not know what she would say about you and Travis and Jonny. She has never been like any other woman. She told me she could never have her own children. She did not have a reason to want to live. Now she has. So have I."

"And what is your reason Raf?"

The boy looks straight at him but waits before replying: "I want you to tell me more about Jesus. I now know about Paul and I like what I know. But what is the problem with Jesus? What will happen to all the Christians if you tell them their God is not a God but merely Jesus who lives close to God?"

Ralph smiles and takes his time to reply. "You must not see that as a problem Raf. You are clearly a thinker and you have the ability to work out things for yourself. That is a gift. The story of Jesus, all the history about what happened before the Cross and all the evidence of what happened on the Cross and afterwards is not just a story about Jesus and who he was. It is a revelation about the most direct, powerful and important message ever delivered to mankind by God. It explains what happens when we die. It also means that Jesus undoubtedly knew before Paul did, what it was like to feel the power of God's presence within himself. There is no record of this in the Bible, except an oblique reference to it in the book of Luke, but no explanation. God also needed Paul to spread the word."

"It is about the next life, in God's spiritual world where we will meet with Him in the ultimate personal experience. It is not complicated. It is about continuous life. That is the right way to approach the story of the Cross. Jesus was the most interesting and wonderful man that ever lived. If you ask me who Jesus was, then I would say he was the Messiah, the number one representative of God on earth. It is a wonderful name, it tells you everything you want to know about him. I am convinced Jesus is very happy at this moment just to be Jesus."

Raf sounds bemused: "But what about God? What about the laws of God and breaking them and what is sin? I believed in Allah because I was afraid of him and I was afraid to die. But I also wanted to die before I discovered there were other rules that would make it impossible to be with my mother. I trusted the Imam because I had no choice. I was prepared to be a martyr because that stopped me from thinking about anything else."

Ralph sounds cautious: "You must learn to take things one at a time. Jesus had an extraordinary close relationship with God. So close he called him Father. But so did Paul call Him Father, and so do I when I am saying my prayers. So will you, I promise, because you will learn he is your best friend as well as your God. And added to this, the real bonus we also have is Jesus as our trusted friend, our guide and our inspiration."

"With Jesus it started early in his life. Religion was important to so many Jews in those days, especially the ones who could not read or write. They always talked about it. We do know Jesus had acquired the skills of reading and writing by the time he started teaching and preaching about life with his Father even though there is no record of anything he had written. The Jews eventually turned the Ten Commandments of Moses into 613 commandments as people tried to work out a way for them to remain as pure as possible. Paul told the world there is only one real perfection, and that is to continue life after death living with God the Father. But Paul accused his Jewish brethren of worshipping a book rather than a real God – a forgiving God, and Jesus became living proof of the wonderful nature of God."

"Before the arrival of Jesus, even the old famous prophets in the Bible did not really appreciate what dying was all about. They trusted their God but they had no real understanding why they prayed to Him. It may be that during those times that is how God preferred his relationship with mortals. The arrival of Jesus meant he changed his plans. Too few people knew there was a Kingdom of God and even fewer knew they had a right to learn how to inherit continuous life."

"In those days there were many Gods available, and many prophets – each with their own ideas, and they all managed to earn a living because people who were able to think for themselves were anxious to learn about a comforting religion. A lot of people suffered with personal demons haunting their private lives."

"Mothers and fathers were always talking about the way one should live and children were encouraged to take part. There was very little writing and even fewer who could read. The Jews were lucky. They had one God that they worshipped and they had the Ten Commandments of Moses engraved on stone. They knew their religion depended on the minds of individuals. Some of the neighbouring tribes adopted the Judean beliefs because it simplified religion. It was all mostly passed on by word of mouth."

"Jesus was very attracted from a young age to the stories of the Old Testament. He had the sort of mind that wanted to know more. There is a record of him going to the Temple when he was about your age and amazing the elders with his knowledge."

"But after that he disappeared until he reappeared as the biblical Jesus with the most wonderful and powerful message about life with his Father after death."

"His reputation frightened those in authority because they recognised his sermons had an authority they knew nothing about and could not challenge."

"Jesus must have had regular communication with his God. This was when he started teaching that relationships with the Father can start on earth. So many Christians fail to appreciate the real meaning of these words."

"And for that reason so many fail to fully grasp the privilege that went to Paul on the road to Damascus. He was alive and well and with both feet firmly anchored to life on earth, when God introduced him to Jesus in his spiritual world. He discovered there was the most powerful link between life on earth and spiritual life afterwards."

Raf is unable to prevent himself from interrupting: "Are you saying continuous life is there for everyone, whoever they are and whatever they do?"

Ralph pauses briefly and chooses his words carefully: "Paul's experience explains how it happens. When we die we enter the spiritual world of God and this is only possible with the help of the power of God's very magnetic presence. Death releases the spirit from the body but continuous life can only be sustained by Gods magnetic presence. If a spirit loses contact with this power it is in very serious trouble. There is no way back – no way for a second chance. We earn our automatic right of making contact through life on earth – and the advice of Jesus. But there is absolutely nothing a spirit can do if it loses contact."

"Sin has a very personal aspect to it. All the things that prevent you from trying to establish a relationship with your God, must be seen as your own personal sin. I think it probably happens often when two people who may well have committed the same sins during their lives, will not both end up close to God. The story of the two men who died with Jesus tells us something very important."

"Are you saying one lost contact on the way to making contact with God? Is that why people pray for dead people?" Raf asks "You're saying for many that must be a waste of time. If you lose contact that's it. There must be many prayers that are a waste of time?"

Ralph is aware that Raf cringes into a smaller bundle on the chair as he continues: "I remember you said that Paul almost lost contact with the powerful light coming from the presence of God. That must be a terrible way to die, to make contact but then to lose it."

The older man looks thoughtfully at the young boy. "Yes Raf – that is exactly right. But remember Paul was alive when it happened to him. What you're saying is right. That is why it is important for friends and relations to be saying their prayers when someone has died. God is not vindictive and he will always help those who have tried to help themselves. He understands and welcomes the power of individuals helping one another throughout life on earth. I believe that is part of his master plan."

"But I don't want you to worry when and if you start reading the bible and especially about Paul. We will take it slowly every day. A lot of what he says needs to be explained. It is called biblical writing."

"You will do exactly what pleases you as I tell you about life in this country for boys your age. This place is not a monastery. It is my home, and also yours. You will decide what you want to do with your life. I will merely explain the options to you. Much is written about a forgiving God and the forgiveness of sins. That means there are a lot of sins to forgive and it is much better in every respect to be in touch with your God on a daily basis. When your time is up there may not be much left to forgive. Don't you think that makes very good sense?"

"When you are ready I will take you to a proper church service. It is essentially always a celebration or should be – remember to see it as such – people getting together and being happy to be in the presence of God. Sometimes the preacher struggles and fails badly to keep his congregation awake, but you must forgive him, because he or she is simply out of their depth."

"Some very beautiful things have been written about our religion, and beautiful music composed. Unfortunately those who edited the Bible, did so to sometimes satisfy their own hopes, needs and expectations rather than to spell it out as it really was. Modern religious thinkers are very un-sophisticated if they ignore the past while trying to explain the present. It's enough to put a lot of people off the Christian religion. These days people need to understand what it is they worship when they attend church on Sundays. They don't like going home with questions unanswered."

"Sin is all around us. It is present in almost everything we do, think about or plan. It controls our minds unless we pray for help in our actions, our plans, our ambitions and our relationships with all those we are in contact with. In other words, we have to learn to live with our sins and for most of us this is not a problem, especially if we learn to pray and ask God for help. Your prayers need only be short. Tell Him exactly what the problem is. Don't try to pray for long periods. God is very busy and very intelligent. Just like people he gets bored if you go on and on and on. Don't call on God for help if you can help yourself. You can pray any time – anywhere. Praying for guidance, for strength, and for understanding and judgement teaches us to think differently and do things differently. We cannot keep ourselves pure because we do not understand what purity is in the eyes of God, and we cannot prevent ourselves from getting involved with life around us. It's a constant battle but it's one no one needs to lose. I am not saying it's OK to indulge yourself in sins providing you keep praying as fast as you can every time you think you have sinned. Don't worry about it. The underlying true values are the same everywhere. It is up to our leaders to make sure this is so."

"It can be a very good life and I will help you in any way you want me to. We can talk about it every day if you like or you can work it out for yourself. I am saying you must be bold and tackle life head on As long as your daily praying stays ahead of your sinning, you're on the right road. But don't think you can pray in advance for a sin you intend to commit. You will never make contact that way. You have to work at it and you will reach a time when you're discovering you're sinning less this week than last week. You begin to acquire an awareness of what you can allow yourself to do and what you want to think about rather than thinking the same as those people around you and doing what you are told to do by others. It is right for people who live in a community to believe in the same values. That is different, but remember your relationship with your God is highly personal."

"If you can discover the magnetic presence of God during your life then your chances of later living close to him are so much better. And the love Jesus spoke about is a great help as you move from one day to the next You can imagine – we are so busy we often have no time to think about God or Jesus. That's when short prayers are such a boon. Otherwise praying becomes a habit rather than a saving refuge. Don't forget God and Jesus know all the tricks. They were there when God told the world that his Kingdom begins on earth."

"If prayer is insincere, you won't make contact. We must make time or else we are in grave danger. God has a sense of humour and one day you'll discover that. But don't worry about it Raf, you'll be all right."

"How do you know that sir?" is Raf's plaintive response.

"I know you want to do the right thing for yourself and for others. That is why you are here sitting next to me asking questions. And I also know you want to meet again with your mother. This is the only way it could happen. If you learn to love your God, the invisible God, this will eventually envelope all your true loves in total safety. That is what heaven and paradise is all about and that is the only thing you can ever be totally certain about."

Chapter Twenty

A massive bank of grey low lying clouds is delaying the arrival of the dawn but the buzzing sound of cars heading in different directions indicates London is awake and early risers are on their way towards their daily tasks. A couple of pedestrians, wearing overcoats for protection against the penetrating damp fresh air briskly walk past St Pauls the Junior, and watching them closely is Travis, about to lift himself over the wall onto the pavement.

The church is lit up as though in anticipation of approaching events.

Travis eases himself onto the pavement and slowly walks towards the lychgate. A front door on the opposite side of the road opens, a man appears and gets into his car and drives away.

In the kitchen Lilah hums a tune as she busies herself laying out the breakfast table with various cereals.

Raf appears in the doorway and she announces: "You have a choice of four cereals and organic eggs and German sausages?"

"What are organic German sausages?"

Lilah's clear laughter resounds through the early morning calm. "Don't be choosy. You're having an international breakfast. The eggs are from the county of Cornwall. You have never had such a breakfast."

"I did yesterday. Travis cooked. He's brilliant."

He sits himself on a stool and says solemnly: "I've had a couple of messages. One asks where you are and the other one asks where I am? They're looking for us."

"I know. I have had the same messages. But it means they don't know where we are."

"I never told them anything."

"I know that. But they know Jonny was responsible for bringing you and your father to this country."

"I've been thinking about that. You spoke to Jonny yesterday. They will do the same today."

Jonny arrives in the doorway. "I seem to be the weakest link."

Ralph arrives and Lilah says: "Travis is walking around the church looking for trouble."

"I saw him go."

"As soon as he gives the clearance, I will leave for the office where I hope to catch the editor before he concentrates on his post. I may not be seeing you people for a while, or until there are further arrests. I'll put my boss in the picture and hopefully he'll help me to make the right decisions."

All pause as they hear the side door open and shut. Travis arrives.

"All clear. But London is stirring."

"Yusuf will be very concerned," Lilah says softly, "and he may wonder if we have been arrested. For them the only alternative to that will be that we have abandoned them. But they won't jump to conclusions. We were a very committed team. There were meetings and discussions and all were very determined and certain they are up for the task."

After a short pause: "There are only three safe houses, and they won't want to lose one. I don't know if they own this one or if it is rented."

"If it's rented they don't have a problem." Travis says.

Lilah nods her agreement: "Yusuf will know of course. He is the brains. He is rich and knows many people including politicians and celebrities. That is how he lives."

"Do you think they will simply abandon it, or if they own it, will they blow it up," Travis asks.

"They do not like to waste resources or money."

"I'll get a couple of men to watch it immediately."

"If anyone visits, it will be Yusuf and he is easy to recognise by his pride and joy, his beard. By now I think they will be alarmed. They don't like to do anything under pressure, and after the shooting in North London they are already under much stress and pressure."

"But it is the movements of the target that will decide when they strike. Everything else is ready. Without us they will have to find replacements. That won't be difficult, but it will take time, and because they won't know for sure what has happened to us, they won't know how close the police are to them? They will be studying the newspapers closer than ever before for information."

Silence prevails as everyone contemplates what she has said.

Then Lilah adds: "I think the most likely thing for them today, is to try to speak to Jonny."

"I rang the office late last night," Jonny says, "and was told there had been a couple of calls from two different men with strange accents – neither left their names but said they would call again."

Lilah sounds thoughtful: "As far as I know they have no contacts with the police so they will be studying the papers to see if there is anything about our arrests."

"Any suggestions," Jonny asks Travis.

"We don't want you on the run, if we can use you."

"You're suggesting using me as bait?" Jonny sounds concerned.

"I'm not making any suggestions. I'm not running the show. If we bring in MI5 they will insist on running the show. And I think they will want to use you somehow. I don't think for a moment they will risk using either Lilah or Raf. The most immediate urgency is to organise a couple of men to watch your flat. I accept what you say that the rest of your former colleagues will be staying out of sight wherever they are, but your flat is the only lead we have. Are there others that Yusuf could use?"

Lilah immediately responds: " They are in contact with another group but they never overlap or work on the same plan. Each one has his own plans to see to. But time for them to do anything is running out. They are under pressure right this moment."

"They will spend today trying to find us, and I feel sure they will phone Jonny. They have his mobile number."

"But yesterday they phoned my office number," Jonny mutters.

"We are not sure it was them. But that fits. We were taught never to use mobiles too often or too long. They know these can be traced."

"I'll be off and I'll be in touch." Jonny says as he departs. " Don't worry, I know a safe route to the office."

With that he leaves.

"Only Yusuf will have a car," Lilah says, "and he would never risk getting personally involved. He has too much to lose."

Travis leaves the kitchen saying: "I'll get ready and go. If I'm early I can wait. We don't have time to waste. The sooner I can get men to watch your flat the better."

Lilah looks concerned. "Please don't be too long."

Her voice fades away. He smiles: "If there is any delay I will let you know. At least for the next few days we must all stay in close touch with one another."

Ralph nods his agreement and looks at his watch: "In the meantime we must plan ahead. I will phone a friend. There is just a possibility that we may have a double celebration today – a baptism followed by a wedding."

Raf is busy eating his cereal after declining the offer of a cooked meal.

"Why are baptisms so important?" he asks.

"Because Christians believe this will alert God, probably through Jesus, and who knows, perhaps Paul will be helping as well as he was the one who started the business of establishing Christian churches. Christians want their God to know that there is a new arrival, a new follower, a new friend, and if it is only a babe, then especially there must be a record "

"What does that mean?"

"It is a sign of faith Raf. We cannot know everything about God's priorities and for that we need faith. We trust Him, to help us to dodge most of the trouble during our daily lives, and also not to cause trouble for other people. We want him to be aware of our children who need our protection. Even Jesus was baptised. We trust God, but that does not mean we expect him to chuck down thunderbolts at our enemies. Babies need special protection."

"We want to prepare Him if tragedy causes one of our children to arrive suddenly and unexpectedly at the door to his Kingdom. It is the pledge we make to our Father that we will look after our children in the best way we can, and that is an extremely important covenant between God and all Christian parents."

"It is the best and most wonderful gift to offer our babies – the first steps towards the Kingdom of God. We want them to be identified immediately on arrival if something goes wrong."

Raf looks very pensive and takes his time.

Lilah says quickly: " To be baptised feels right to me Raf. Things are happening very quickly for us and I like that. Already I am feeling a freedom I have never known before. We are starting a new life."

"Like Paul?" he asks.

She nods. "Yes, and like him we can have a new name. A new name will protect us against our enemies. Yusuf and his men are now our enemies."

"Being baptised a Christian is the most revolutionary thing we could do, even if Yusuf will never know, but it might have been better if he did. It would tell him we are not the same people he once knew."

"You will be known as Lilah and Raf from Copsem Gardens in London, the first to be baptised here since I moved in," Ralph says, "and as a Christian I believe the heavens will rejoice when they hear the new names."

Lilah looks thoughtfully at Raf: "I would like to choose a new name for myself. It will be Jennifer, and friends will call me Jenny. I once knew a very gentle English girl called Jenny, on holiday in Jerusalem. I want to become as gentle a she was. Travis will help me. He is a very gentle and considerate and kind man."

Raf sounds troubled: "I have a problem sir with what you have just said. I have always believed my mother is safe with Allah living like a princess in her big house, with many servants. If I arrive at the paradise of your God, how will I find my mother? And if I have a new name that will be make it impossible. Even if somehow she is able to find her way to the new paradise, and she knocks on the door, who will she ask for?"

When Ralph remains thoughtfully silent he continues: "They will tell her she is at the wrong place. I will be new. Perhaps Jesus and Paul will know about me but how will they know about my mother? She was never baptised and it sounds as though paradise must be a very big place."

Ralph is silent as he looks at the back of the church.

Raf continues hopefully: "Unless it happens with her the way it happened with Paul. Is that possible sir? At first Paul, on the Damascus Road could not recognise the power of God's light, and he almost lost contact. If my mother does not recognise the light of the new God, your God, then will she have enough time to work it out for herself – the way Paul did, or was he a quick thinker sir? My Mother always needed time to think about her problems. Many times she asked me to listen when she prayed. She always tried to make deals with Allah, because she felt she could not really trust our Imam. He changed his mind about things from week to week, the worse the war became the more he wanted to punish everyone and anyone he was in contact with."

"Is your God patient as well as a forgiving God sir?"

Ralph faces the boy and says gently: " Now you know why Christians like to remind God about loved ones that have died – just in case it helps.

"But don't worry about waiting in paradise. There are no clocks."

"The more I listen to you Raf, the more I see and hear your mother, and I like her."

"Perhaps if she could have trusted her Imam more she may have been able to think through her problems much quicker."

"But from this moment on, Raf, you must accept that there is only one paradise for everybody, from all the nations on earth. It is up to each individual to work out for him or herself how to inherit the grace to enter. Unfortunately most people are let down by their religious leaders. In this country we have the same problems."

He watches the boy's expression closely, but there is no indication what impact his words may have had. Then Raf says slowly: "There must be more than one door to knock on sir for when you want to enter the

Kingdom of God? Think of all the people dying every day, every hour, every minute, everywhere, from different religions."

He stops and looks expectantly at Ralph. Relief shows in his eyes when the older man smiles. "I don't think doors are a problem Raf, but it is a very interesting thought. Are you thinking there should be different doors for different religions or are you thinking Christians need to tell more people about Jesus and Paul?"

Silence as Raf contemplates the suggestion. Then he asks softly: "Do you think it is possible sir that other religions can get into your God's paradise."

"Not if they don't believe in Jesus on the Cross, Raf, and God's role in what had happened and how it happened. The crucifixion provided God with an ideal opportunity to reveal his power and to explain that paradise is for ordinary people like you and me – all the peoples on earth, should they have the will to discover how to inherit this gift. If you don't look for God through Jesus or Paul, you may not find him. I can't say it will be impossible because I cannot speak for God. Jesus warned against false prophets. He is still warning against them."

"Christians believe that those who tamper with the nature of God are trying to create a God in their own image rather than the other way. We know we are created in His image, and that means we have a spirit inside us. But we are given free wills to make our own decisions. We also know some of us are born into very difficult circumstances. When we first open our eyes we are surrounded by powerful influences – not just those of our parents. That should be reason enough for Christians to want to have their babies baptised as soon as possible."

"When we leave this world we are immediately confronted by God's presence in his spiritual world but if the spiritual life within us is underdeveloped, weak and without purpose it will not recognise the magnetic power of this Presence. You may think it strange to speak of magnetic power and then not being able to recognise it but that in a nutshell is God's righteousness. It is also the secret of life. It is the same for people living anywhere and everywhere. If you become a politician you may wish to contradict what I have just said, but then, that will be your problem. It will not be the problem of my God, or Jesus or Paul."

"But don't worry about it. I have been giving you a lot of information quickly. We are all under pressure and I am trying to help you and Lilah to understand if you wish to live here with me, you will be free to make your own choices. I am telling you about Paul and Jesus in order that you may discover what it is like to have a loving and forgiving God as your friend."

" It can be said that everything you read in the Bible leads to the crucifixion of Jesus. The best information I can give you is to start with the Cross. Put aside the details of the early life of Jesus. Concentrate on the crucifixion. That is what Paul did – life after Jesus with Jesus."

"If we have difficulty in finding Jesus, we have Paul to help us. He is one of us. He was a sinner who was forgiven. If he was able to find Jesus through God, then so can you and so can I. Even your Imam has the same chance providing he stops preaching about a nasty and vindictive God. I would not advise you to go back and try to convert him – don't even think about it !"

"If you like, just to start off, we can pray together. I will teach you how to pray the right way. It is no big deal. I won't be trying to replace your mother. I cannot do that. I will simply help you to be honest with yourself and if you are, you will also be honest with your God, and then you will get on very well with one another."

He pauses and watches as the boy grapples with a thought: "I would like you to teach me how to be honest with myself sir. That is something my mother forgot to explain."

"It is nothing to be too concerned about Raf. For now just teach yourself to relax completely. Your life is going to be very different on a day to day basis."

"We'll do everything gradually at your own pace and I promise your relationship with God will become closer and much more secure."

"Don't worry about your mother. If you think she is waiting for you, she won't mind. I can't promise she is watching over you, because, if she is with my God, and I think there may just be a good chance she is, she will know you are doing your best for yourself and the people you love. That is what every mother would wish for her children – to inherit the gift of Gods grace, because ultimately He decides who will be drawn into life with Him. Even if it feels you are not doing enough to deserve to go to paradise, just remember how Paul, despite all the tribulations, disappointments and losing battles, held on to the truth all through his life."

"There were days when he felt very low and said it was as though he had died a hundred times that day. That was simply because most of the people he met that day refused to become part of the new way of living he had gone to great pains to explain to them. Being rejected made him very unhappy because he knew he was offering individuals the greatest news they could ever hope to receive."

"Getting baptised means taking the first step in the right direction."

This time Raf responds immediately: "I will be very pleased to take the second name of Duncan sir, but to play safe I will hold on to the name I know my mother will recognise."

Ralph smiles again: "I am sure that is very acceptable Raf."

Then he turns to Lilah: " I have a feeling that you may have a problem as well Lilah?"

She nods. "It is something you said last night. Muslims have always said that Jesus was just a prophet and not a God. Are you now saying the same? So have they been right all the time?"

After taking a few steps away he turns to look from Lilah to Raf and back again. "No Lilah they have not been right. Those who make this claim, reveal they have no understanding of God's role in what happened on the Cross and afterwards. The truth about the Cross is about God's creative powers at work, while having to cope with the opposing collective will powers of human beings. The miracle of the Cross is not a story about the supernatural powers of Jesus, it is a straightforward example of the nature of God's influence and power. I feel reluctant to speak of Jesus, before the crucifixion, as being the Son of God, but I certainly have no hesitation, after the crucifixion, to refer to him as the Spiritual Son of God. That was most assuredly how Paul saw Jesus in the spiritual world of God."

"And that is what the spiritual Jesus means to me. He is as real, certain and recognisable as anything I can see or understand on earth."

"I also believe Paul knew Jesus experienced similar manifestations to the one he had had on the road to Damascus. That may be why Paul hardly ever referred to the work of Jesus during his teachings and sermons. He wanted to set Jesus apart because he was the first to be drawn into continuous life in the new Covenant with God, and to Paul that meant he had to be the spiritual Son of God."

"Paul never saw himself as the equal of Jesus, and he always made sure that everyone he spoke to understood that. He saw his role for God as different from what Jesus was asked to do. There is no record of him calling Jesus the Spiritual Son immediately after his Damascus Road experience. That may be because Paul at first thought it had been a physical resurrection because, in his previous life as a Pharisee, that is what he had believed – that God would reward those who had lived "pure lives" with a physical resurrection at the end of time."

"Almost all the Jews of that time believed in such a resurrection and that is one of the huge changes that the life of Jesus brought to mankind. It is not known exactly when Paul understood that indeed he had been introduced to the Spiritual Jesus. It took him time to mature into his new identity of being Paul instead of Saul. We know Paul experienced other manifestations. He said so although the others may not have been of the same character and strength as the first"

"And of course, this introduced a crucial difference to the way he spoke about the promise of continuous life. It may be this is what confused Luke and other historians of the time who wrote about Paul's "indescribable experience as having been caused by a flashing light". Luke may not have understood what spiritual life was and how immediately Judgement Day was available for every person who departed from life on earth."

"Christians today still suffer from the same confusion and they have to look to their leaders who refer to God and Jesus both as the Lord. It is right to state categorically that the Holy Spirit and the very essence of Jesus is part of God. It is very fitting that the very best that humanity can offer, should be a part of God's nature. But it is not correct to call Jesus God. Never lose track of the fact that only God the Father has power over life and death. Modern day Christians as well as Muslims should demand clarity from their leaders."

"Newcomers to Christianity are turned away by the claim that Jesus was a supernatural God. Sophistication has taken control of religious habits."

" The Jews were just about the most persecuted tribe of all time, under occupation often enough, on the losing end of many wars, they were dispersed over different lands. When Jesus arrived he was welcomed as the Messiah, the Son of God but there were also those who hoped he would be the mythological Christ on his mighty steed and wielding his indestructible sword who would lead their armies to drive the Romans back to Rome. Above all the Jews wished for a world with no wars, no hatred and no sin. They were emphatically a subjugated tribe."

"Add to his reputation his ability as a healer, and as an inspirational speaker, and people walked for many miles to attend the meetings of Jesus. For the poor and the oppressed he brought a wonderful message of hope, charity and love. But even some of the wealthy ones, and those wanting to drive the Romans out of Judea were drawn to listen to him. His growing popularity worried the authorities in Jerusalem, both the Romans and the intellectuals who were out of their depth trying to understand what the meaning was of the New Kingdom."

"Surely God would have known that sending a supernatural being would not have been right for His cause. Jesus had to be seen to be human or else the story of the Cross would have had a totally different meaning and would have ended up buried deep in Jewish religious mythology. And it is extremely doubtful we would ever have heard of the Pharisee called Saul."

"Jesus represents every human being who wants to be drawn into Gods Kingdom and what really happened on the Cross is available to every individual everywhere. The Bible says Jesus was free from sin. He may well have been. For those who live close to God, often have absolutely no interest in living the way other people live. Paul was a married man."

"To become a Pharisee, marriage was essential. That was the culture. We don't know what happened to Paul's wife, but we do know Paul admits he became a celibate. He clarified this saying that is what matters to those like him who spend their lives working for God. They simply do not have the time or inclination to contemplate living any other way."

"But that must not detract from the fathers of today. Family life is part of God's master plan. Christians, most of the time, make very good parents."

"Jesus was known to kiss Mary Magdalene on her lips every time she joined him and his group, causing one or two to ask if that meant Jesus loved her more than them?"

"Jesus felt concerned about the way people saw him and thought about him and he is quoted in the Bible asking several individuals if they thought he was the Messiah or the Son of God? Jesus was looking ahead to the future when he would not be around and he was concerned that the promise of Life from his Father should be carried on by his disciples and also those that they converted after that and onwards into posterity."

"He was aware that his presence was causing concern to some authorities in Jerusalem, and he knew there was a warring section among his followers who expected and wanted different leadership from him."

"His entrance into Jerusalem proved just how concerned he was. It not only testified to his wonderful moral courage, and trust in his Father, it exemplified the immense love he felt for those who followed him, and who lined the streets to welcome him."

"It was the time of Pass Over - a very famous religious celebration. There were to be many thousands of religious Jews and others travelling to Jerusalem for the occasion. His supporters wanted him to be there, and he saw it as a wonderful opportunity to speak to much larger congregations."

"But he must have thought hard and carefully about it and he decided to send an important message to those who wanted to welcome him as the Christ."

"He asked for a donkey to carry him into the city."

"The streets were lined with people who laid palm leaves to honour his arrival."

"But for those looking for a general to conquer the Romans, their cheers changed to jeers and when they heard him speak of love, and forgiveness the jeers became an angry crescendo. When Pontius Pilate gave them the choice between Jesus and Barabbas the murderer, their frustrations made them choose Jesus to be crucified. They wanted Roman blood, and they started by taking the blood of Jesus. Little did they know how their treachery would resound into history."

"But we know of course that God used the horrendous disaster to deliver the most vital message to mankind about continuous life."

"Jesus had made no attempt to defend himself but he did declare that his kingdom was not from this world. His wonderful news that the Kingdom of God started on earth had been distorted by his intellectual enemies and some of his misguided supporters into sounding that he had arrived to become the new King of the Jews to lead their armies against the Romans."

"Jesus knew that words about love and forgiveness would not be enough to prevent what was taking place during his trial and he resigned himself to allow his Father to take control."

"Nowhere does the sheer humanity of Jesus reveal itself so powerfully as during those brutal moments on the Cross when the sheer agony of a very slow painful physical demise, challenged his human vulnerability forcing him to cry out: "My God my God why have You forsaken me?"

"For the man who understood God's power better than any other man on earth, the man who had felt the protective power of God's presence in his body, and who trusted his father with such unquestioned simplicity and devotion, that was a heart rending submission of his physical mortality."

"Even he felt very briefly trapped by a desolate fear that something had gone wrong?"

Ralph pauses and his voice lowers to a whisper: "Nothing had gone wrong, but his human frailty was heard and witnessed by all those who had gathered round – some perhaps hoping for a very late miracle, while the others were there to gloat over the man who had been described by some followers as the next King of the Jews."

"Jesus did not die. We know that at some moment God moved closer to enable the power of his presence to set free the spirit of Jesus into paradise. We do not know exactly when this happened, but we know it did."

Raf blinks as he looks at Ralph. Then he asks softly: "Sir, was the Spiritual Jesus the same spirit that belonged to the other Jesus?"

Ralph smiles: "I can see what you're thinking Raf......."

The boy chooses his words carefully: "If the Spiritual Jesus was the same Spirit as in the physical Jesus, then why can't both be the Son of God?"

"I agree with you Raf," the older man says gently, "They are the same, and if you want to call Jesus the Son of God I will not disagree with you, providing you don't claim he was God or that he had the powers of God. He was a very special and gifted man and he undoubtedly must have had help from God while spreading the news of continuous life into His Kingdom. The story of the Cross must he looked upon as a manifestation of God's forgiving grace. It was not about the identity of Jesus. We know who Jesus was. His reply to Pontius Pilate at his trial made it absolutely clear what Jesus was all about, and what the New Kingdom meant – it was about life with his Father in a different life – a spiritual life. His teachings, his sermons, his news was about life with his Father in God's Kingdom. For further clarity we have to thank Paul. We don't know why Luke and other writers lost track or tried to disguise the real facts, for whatever reason, while introducing the new Christian religion. False prophets abounded. I wonder if it would not have been better to refer to this new religion as the Followers of Jesus, or the Followers of the Messiah. It is perhaps ironic that we are known as Christians? But names don't concern me. I'm happy to call myself a Christian."

Silence prevails as both Lilah and Raf contemplate what they had just heard. Raf is sitting in his favourite position with both knees tucked up under his chin. Lilah's soft eyes remain fixed on the older man who expectantly looks straight back at her. Her voice is steady and even as she says softly: "What you say has the ring of truth about it, but I feel disappointed, as I am sure most Christians would feel had they been listening to you. A supernatural Jesus promises protection and great comfort You have just said that there were no miracles. Does that mean we have to fight our own battles, rely on our wits and whatever means to survive, and the hope that sometimes Jesus will manage to get his Father to do something when we least expect it."

Ralph moves his eyes to the boy who waits expectantly and then returns to her.

"What I am saying Lilah is that the miracles mentioned in the Bible can be divided into two different kinds."

"There were those used by writers and historians to proclaim Jesus as a super natural God, and there were those that were very decisively attached to what God was attempting to achieve on earth. This probably happened because the writers did not fully understand what the Crucifixion was all about."

"We have to decide which of the two happened as part of God's will, and which happened to soothe the inadequacies of those who wrote about Jesus and Paul? It is not a difficult decision for me to make because it does not make sense for me to believe Jesus was supernatural in order to believe what happened on the Cross."

"It is much more acceptable to choose the miracles that helped God to spread his wonderful message about continuous life with him, away from the physical expectations of all the generations before and after the Event."

"It is quite possible that Paul remained confused in his own interpretation of what had happened to himself, and he decided to correct this by spreading the news that the Second Coming of Jesus was going to happen in his lifetime. He said this as an answer to what the fervent belief had been up until then – that all those who had lived pure lives, would be physically resurrected at the end of time, the end of the world, to claim their inheritance next to God. Paul could no longer believe in that. What would have been the point of physical resurrection if this happened at the end of time and the end of the world, and so he shortened the time span of expectation, claiming it was going to happen in his lifetime."

"We know that did not happen."

Chapter Twenty-one

The relentless tick-tock of the large grandfather clock directly in front of him has become a very comforting sound to Raf. Of all the new sounds that are now part of his new life, it is the one that personifies a fresh continuity and reassurance and at nightime it helps to put him to sleep. But he also knows it reminds him that Ralph is in the next room, and that Travis and Jenny are below. And every time he says a short prayer it is always to ask God to allow life to continue as it is.

His hands fumble his mobile as he restlessly waits for it to announce that Jonny Singer has received his message. The longer he waits the more he feels certain something has gone wrong and the fear grows it may develop into a matter of life and death.

He has not told the others about his anxiety and forboding ever since he received his latest message saying: "We have been talking to your friend Jonny Singer and we have told him we have a great story for him, and that we should all meet together to talk about it. You and Lilah have a great conbribution to make."

A soft shuffle behind him makes him jump to his feet, and he heaves a deep sigh of relief when he sees Ralph, wearing his nightgown.

"I'm sorry, I did not want to startle you. Can't you sleep?"

Raf looks at the mobile in his hands.

"You've got another message!"

Raf nods:"I think Jonny is in trouble. I have been trying to get to him."

Ralph takes the mobile reads and looks at the boy.

Raf whispers:"Jonny must not meet them anywhere except in his office, and he must not meet with one person alone. That could be a disaster. They will try to lure him somewhere. Then they will put a belt around him and he will be lost, and so will we. They will force him to bring them here."

"How long is it since you sent him the message??"Over two hours...."

"He may be on a job?"

Raf nods, looking troubled.

"Can I sit here and wait with you. If it's a problem, then it's a problem for both of us." Raf nods, and watches as he moves a chair closer.

"You have a lot of things on your mind – try to think of things one at a time, and don't hesitate to ask questions."

"Don't think that you are caught between two religions. There is only one God for everyone but millions haven't a clue who he is, and others prefer a very distorted version of the One God. I don't think it will take you long to become a Christian once you realise just how peaceful it is compared to being a militant fanatic from any other religion. But in the modern Western World there are minority groups who are fighting to turn Jesus against his Father, and some Christians quite clearly do not believe in God. Now that's a bit of nonsense I hope you can easily avoid making contact with. It has everything to do with the freedom that some believe is what Democracy affords them and it has nothing to do with the Love of God. Paul faced exactly the same problems with his early converts"

The response is so swift it surprises Ralph.

"I am not worried about leaving Allah sir, but I am a bit worried about your God, and Jesus. I like Paul."

"What is it that worries you ?"

" It's the forgiveness of sin sir. How will I know if your God forgives me? Will I get a sign of some sort. I need to know sir. How much does He forgive and does He forgive everything I have done? And how will I let my mother know? And if Jonny is used to kill many people, will I be forgiven for that, because it will be my fault"

There is a long pause as Raf holds his breath in anticipation. Ralph makes him wait, and then he looks deep into his eyes as he says:

"God did not create sin Raf. That would be a ridiculous accusation. Neither did God create a devil called Satan. Neither did God create Gabriel the Arch Angel. These were props used by the preachers of that time, to help people to understand the difference, as it was perceived at the time, between the right way to live and the wrong way to live. Your main battle is not with God or Jesus, but with yourself. The sin you fear was created by yourself and those around you, and ahead of you. You need Jesus to guide you. God deals with everything connected to life with Him or death. We trust he is aware of the condition of souls and spirits but, because he did not create sin, it is very doubtful he keeps a acomputer handy to check what we're up to on a daily basis. Don't misunderstand this Raf, it does not mean God is overstretched and it does not mean there are gaps through which evil and other demonstrably unsuitable spirits can sneak into the next life.The entire operation – meaning moving from this life into the next is far less complicated than what most people imagine it to be. In all probability most spirits already know on arrival if they have any hope of hanging onto the magnetic presence of God. If you don't look for the real one God in this life, you are unlikely to find Him in the next."

Raf sounds troubled: "You're saying not all the main gods are the same god sir?"

Ralph's response is gentle: "How can it be so Raf. Think about it. Not even all the Christians worship the same god. Many, even leaders, merely pay lip service."

"The experience of Paul tells us everything we need to know. The biggest mistake that many Christian leaders make is to preach that it was Jesus who spoke to Paul when a voice said to Paul on the Demascus road 'Why are you persecuting me?'

"That could not have been Jesus. He does not have the power. It was the power of the light eminating from God's presence that took possession of Paul's entire being. Then Jesus appeared standing in front of the cross. Paul immediately knew he was looking at Jesus, even though he had never met him or seen him before. The very same light that had taken possession of his own body and mind, was also connected to Jesus. But it was God who spoke."

"Paul was in a state of Grace and he was speechless."

"It was only several days after this when Paul understood that God had forgiven him his sins. Or else He would surely not have manifested in the way he did and spoken to him. And for several days Paul wandered about like a blind man, filled with wonder, awe and fear. He realised his life leading up to his revelation had been spent in a monstrous manner. He understood clearly the meaning of God's words – 'if you persecute Jesus and his followers, you're also persecuting Me.'

"And that is when Paul knew what he had to do."

"Many times after that he felt compelled to tell his converts, that even though he hoped and prayed that he would one day again feel the presence of God within himself, that it would only happen through.the Grace of God. Even Paul had his moments when he wondered if he would really be forgiven for the life he had led before that wonderful experience on the Damascus road. That uncertainty became his strength, and drove him to become the man that walked thousands of miles into sometimes hostile situations as he sought to get individuals to understand the power of his message about the living Jesus. Paul never took his conversion for granted and even his successes did not make him feel complacent."

Ralph is aware that Raf is still bemused and he adds softly: "That is why you need faith Raf. What happened to Paul may never happen to you but if you live life in the Spirit of what really happened on the Cross, and also on the Damascus road with Paul then your chances of actually finding yourself drawn into the presence of God, either in this life or the next is so much stronger."

"You must push aside your current religious beliefs and start again. It should not be too difficult because you wont have to start at the beginning. There are things both religions have in common. Even if you doubt you can cope with the challenge – think, the benefit to you will be really quite spectacular. For you it would almost be like a resurrection. Open your mind to the love of God as taught by Jesus and Paul and you will learn to elevate your thoughts above everything happening to you."

"Don't be afraid of your doubts, your questions, or troubles – discuss them with your new Father – the more often you do this, the higher your understanding and appreciation will become how to cope with it.."

"This is what happened to the disciples after the Crucifixion when they were in a state of shocked disbelief, despair, fear, a sence of deprivation, loneliness and confusion. For those who were able to pray for help, there followed wonderful relief. God gave them the power to see Jesus for long enough to appreciate that he was alive. God not only felt obliged to intervene in this way, he could see that the New Covenant he had forged with Jesus was going to be challenged and the disciples needed confirmation to take their thought processes to a higher level. But it was not the physical Jesus he allowed them to see, it was the spiritual Jesus, looking absolutely identical to the other one."

"This was not the same experience that would happen to Paul later on. That would have confused the disciples completely. God simply gave them the power to see for themselves that Jesus was alive. That may have been when He realised He would have to introduce Paul or a Paul at a future time."

"There was no specific continuity about these manifestations by Jesus, nor do we know what the time span was. The way it happened makes it impossible for a group of disciples to have had the experience at the same moment. It happened individually. That is the way God has chosen throughout the centuries to maintain his influence on the direction taken by mankind. If that feels tenuous Raf, then it should give you an idea of the divine power Paul encountered on the road to Damascus – it was massive, almost indescribable. All these events undoubtedly made this the most powerful period of spiritual manifestations since God created human life."

"Such was the religious chaos of the times God understood the message of Jesus might be lost in the aftermath of the Crucifixion."

"It is absolutely crucial that the Christian message must be that the disciples had seen the spiritual Jesus or else the real message of the Resurrection would be damaged."

"Paul's greatest joy on his travels was when he was told converts had really understood what was meant by life in the spirit and how they remained faithful. Equally, he felt he had failed when told converts had reverted to their sinful ways."

"This taught him that perfection was only achievable when a spirit was drawn into the presence of God, and that the Grace of God was such a crucial ally of Faith. It caused him to admit to some of his closest companions that the Damascus experience alone was not enough for him to feel absolutely secure he would again feel the power of his Father's presence, in this life or the next."

"But that doesn't mean you must live life in a monastry Raf. It does mean you must save time for your God while you get on with earning a living, and making the right choices for yourself in the life you wish to live."

"If that doesn't sound easy, it isn't and wont be, which is why it is better to have parents, one of each, and friends, and in particular a strong relationship with the One God we all believe in. Now you know why it is so important to understand why it is so crucial to resist the temptations that will undermine your relationship with God's loving, caring and trusting nature."

He takes a deep breath before continuing: "Paul spent most of his life after his Damascus Experience with his new churches talking on a one to one basis to people about the way they should live. He tried to understand individual problems into the smallest detail. He knew many individuals created demons in their own minds. With some, these demons became so strong, they turned into a personal devil that took control and this forced those individuals to self- destruct. It was a gigantic task and challenge because it put one will against another, except in Paul's case. He spoke from a platform of having had the ultimate experience that provided all his subsequent wisdom and insight. It was a tremendous disappointment to him, causing him grief, when he understood that most of the Jews he was in contact with at the time, failed to appreciate that his experience underlined the message brought to the Jewish nation and the world about life with God after death."

"But the Jewish inability to simply adjust to a reality that was divinely undeniable became the gain of the rest of the world. Paul started preaching to the gentiles, and that effectively deprived the Jewish nation of the right to claim they were God's specially chosen nation. To this day they have not forgiven Paul for this."

"Paul would be the first to concede that there is a sophistication in existence now that must be taken into consideration, providing individuals do not attempt to interfere with the nature and character of the God that created mankind. And the way to do this is to follow God's manifestation of love from the Crucifixion back to the beginning of time when there must have been very close contact between the early humans and the Holy Spirit This is impossible to deny, because human life would have imploded very early on without the presence of God's love and guidance. In the life of the western world it is a fact that the strength of democratic freedom is also its weakness. It is a freedom a long distance from the freedom Paul tried to help his converts to discover."

"Just think of all the wonderful gifts you were born with Raf – you can see, hear, speak, think, feel, enjoy – you have hands, arms and legs to help and many more amazing attributes – mostly unseen and these are by far the more important because they form part of your spirit. But think what a problem it must have been for Adam and Eve, and the others during those very early days. God's Holy Spirit must have worked overtime, as humans walked about trying to make sense of themselves and what to do about hunger, danger, not having homes, and walking about without the protection of clothes. People are still walking about today wondering what to do with their lives and how to fill all the empty spaces their spirits are aware of. There are many more false prophets and devils today selling their fraudulent ideas and dreams "

"Life today is not far removed from then, except that today babies are born to parents who welcome them, and from the day they are born, they start to learn. They are not born in sin, they are born in love- God's love, and the love of their parents. But they soon drift into the lives of their parents, and their environment. If they are fortunate they will have a father as well as a mother to provide balance to their way of tackling growing up."

"During those early days, guided by the Holy Spirit, and taken from one adventure to the next, they discovered new things every day. It is still like that. Even in those days groups of people would have discovered life is better as a community, helping one another and travelling in the same direction, with the love of God. But with life's experiencess and self confidence came sophistication, bravado, and gradually the power of individual free wills led to a parting of the ways from the earlier times when the Holy Spirit inspired their deliberations, conscience and decision making."

"God watched, waited and then decided to do something about it. Jesus arrived and a bit later Paul. But there were many splinter groups after the Crucifixion determined they knew best and the chaos that existed before Jesus arrived continued for sometime after his physical removal from earth. God is not on record saying Jesus had died for our sins. He left that to Paul to explain."

"There were many human disasters during the times spanning the Old Testament and gradually people started hoping for a better way to understand life. They began to yearn for news, events, to uplift their spirits but they struggled, because they had lost contact with the love of God, and to compensate they began to believe in different gods to help them. They still believed that there had to be a higher power, but they thought various things like powerful animals, high mountains and other things free from the influence of human nature, was worth acknowledging as deity. The Israelis were the same but they were the only ones where some clung to all the wise bits handed down by their forefathers and when God felt he should trust what he saw he used the Holy Spirit to once again influence events."

"There were many famous biblical gloom and doom prophets to warn Israel that further catastrophies lay ahead unless they returned to the ways of their fathers. But the reports we have of life all that long ago, show no proper understanding of the loving nature of God, nor does it give any indication that any of the prophets knew anything about spiritual life and life in the spirit"

"When Jesus told people to think differently and to do things differently he really meant we should all get back to living with the love of God. By all means do whatever we want to do to earn a living, but do not shut out the God of Jesus and Paul – the Crucifixion tells two stories, one is about the wonderful nature of God, and the other is that not everyone will be welcome when they die. God emphasised this when he said to Paul: 'Why are you persecuting me?'

"The god of militant terrorists is a very vindictive and punishing god, created by those who need a figurehead to answer to all their own devillish demands. You must choose Raf. I believe you have already done that. Now you must be strong. You could become a great leader for your nation, if you can help get everyone on the same motorway leading to the Kingdom of the Father of Jesus, and that begins here on earth. You have a very unique and wonderful story to tell, and one of the great discoveries coming to you, is when you find out just how wonderful this God of Jesus and Paul is. You're not alone. A large majority of the people of this country are just as lost and confused as you were a few weeks ago. Modern Christianity has evolved into a nanny religion with people expecting God to be at their beck and call and if he cannot prevent death and disease and wars and criminality, and poverty then he is seen as a powerless god not worth a second thought."

"It is easy to understand why Jesus started his ministry talking to the poorest and the oppressed – because they were the ones who needed comfort beyond the experience and appreciation of the sophisticated, rich and famous. Theirs was the gift of immediately.grasping what Jesus and Paul was bringing to them."

Raf sounds very unsure of himself: "How can I prove to your God I want to be different, and reborn like Paul and you sir. Will your God reveal himself to me in the same way?"

Ralph lowers his eyes and his voice: "The only way I can answer that is to ask you not to expect to be rewarded for what you do Raf. Don't even think about it. When you least expect it, then it may happen to you. God does sometimes reply in the most amazing manner to very urgent calls, but we must not think we deserve it. Dying is normal. Getting ill is also inevitable. If you get run over by a bus, it could be your own fault. The fact that I can hear the need in you to live a different life, to me is proof that God has heard you. Keep an open mind, and if you like, work with me. For the time being we'll forget about going to school. You can already read and you can write – better than most of the people Jesus was in contact with during his time. Until you feel ready to face the new world – and you have decided what sort of life you want, don't worry about it. When you are ready you will know."

After a slight pause he continues: "Just think how wonderful it must have been in the beginning to have had the Holy Spirit working through the instincts, senses and courage of the first people as a guide on a daily basis to start getting on with fulfilling the hopes and wishes of God the Father."

He holds up an admonishing finger: "Don't ask me when it all started going wrong Raf and don't ask who created the word sin for all those who preferred to do it themselves and go their own way. There were no early priests until the wills of men and women decided to take the crooked, difficult, thorny and very life threatening road away from the highway leading to the Love of God."

"It may all have begun somewhere not too far away from Jerusalem. I believe God favoured those who lived in the surrounding areas of Galilee down to Jerusalem. The history we have records of, prove decisively that the nomads who collectively became known as the Israelis, your ancestors, were a very talented, intelligent, and intrinsically loyal kind of people - they were also almost destroyed by foreign armies on so many occasions ".

"Jerusalem was raised to the ground 20 times. Even so, the indestructible spiritual links born in each of us survived among the generations who were conquerred, enslaved and dispersed to foreign lands. Creation stands as proof of God's patience and it was surely the role of the women to pass on the tales of valour, belief, origin and expectations of a better life while they were living in exile. They kept alive the hopes of a new life with aspirations of a peaceful existence, and when the Babylonians were defeated, the new conquerors, the Persians, allowed what was left of the 10,000 top ranked and very influential Israelis they had taken captive under Nebudkanezzer to return to the land of their birth if they wanted to. It is testament to the indestructability of the human spirit in partnership with the Holy Spirit that the Israellis should have prevailed all the disasters."

" Then, some 450 years before the arrival of Jesus a priest called Ezra decided to gather all the history, and mythological stories into one book. The Five chapters of Moses became the Old Testament, and Deuteronomy became the most influential document ever written in the history of the world - a book that virtually formed the Western World as we know it today. This book was written, not by the wealthy, intellectual or successful, but was produced collectively by the ordinary farm peasants in Juda who were the first to settle into a communal way of life. Eventually they formed the first government, and became a nation to which people could belong if they knew how to write and read. This led to the formal declaration that there was only one God and from then on all evidence of any earthly gods was forcefully demolished and removed. About 200 years before Jesus arrived, we find the first signs that spiritual life, the survival of the soul, was beginning to enter into the minds of those who in their own way had made contact again with the Holy Spirit."

"One thing I can promise you with confidence Raf, is that God is on your side. Paul said very confidently when he heard that his Jewish enemies had gone to some of his churches to rubbish what he had preached about his Damascus Road experience, that 'God proved he was on my side on the road to Damascus and with God by my side, who dares to challenge me and why should I care how manifold my enemies are, and what they might try and do to me. I see death as a gain.'

Pause, as the penny drops:"Of course you already have that in common with Paul , because you want to join your mother."

"Yes sir, but I must be sure I will knock on the right door."

"I could not have put it better myself Raf. You have a very good memory. Even I can't recall all the things I have told you and Jenny since you have moved into my home. I was so anxious for you to understand that your religion is not all that far removed from those who are Christian. We do not need guns and bombs to remove those differences. I believe Mohammed borrowed facts from the history of the Jews to show how close the nations really are. There is nothing wrong with that. It is just unfortunate that he did not understand the truth about Jesus and Paul."

" I already believe that sir. But I know I have a lot of other things to think about." Ralph nods his agreement.

The side door opens and Travis enters, followed by Jenny.

Raf turns,and says: "We are waiting for Jonny to contact me."

At that moment his mobile rings sharply, and when Raf reads the message, he breathes deeply and says: "He got my message sir, and he says he is also talking to MI5." Travis nods his agreement."I was informed about this, but I waited for further news before telling you about it."

"Did I miss anything?" Jenny asks.

Ralph smiles. "We had a short crisis but you are just in time to hear what sounds like hopeful news. And as we are all together perhaps we should toast our hopes that this could resolve your problems. Any details you can tell us about?"

Travis looks hesitant before saying: "We're confident we can use the fact that Jonny proved his sympathetic approach to the Palestinians cause when he brought Raf and his father into the UK."

He walks towards the kitchen asking: 'red or white sir?'

Jenny chips in quickly:"Can I please have white, especially if it's bubbly?"

Then she takes a seat next to Raf and says:" If Raf and I are going to become Christians, should we start reading your Bible, and if we do, perhaps we should do it together so we can talk."

Ralph interrupts: "I hope I can join these sessions, and we'll start with the good news – the New Testament and the story of Jesus. From there it is much easier to appreciate The Old Testament. There are records, even though the 150 authors of the Bible sometimes wrote in very mysterious ways. By looking very closely at Paul, we will get to know Jesus much better. There were many false prophets at that time, selling their ideas and copying whatever someone like Paul might have said. That may be why Paul, or was it Luke, who made the decision, that his Damascus experience should be referred to as an 'event that was indescribable'? It is a fairly modern development that the churches in this country have, somewhat reluctantly, opened their minds to accept that life with God means spiritual life, without the body as we know it."

Travis returns with drinks on a tray and a coke for Raf. After taking a sip Raf asks: "I remember you saying you disagree with some of things written in the Bible sir?"

Ralph in turn takes a slow sip and then says softly: "I don't disagree with the gist of the messages Raf, just the way it was written. A very good example of this is the report in John's Gospel about the raising of Lazarus. It was undoubtedly the most important biblical miracle of Jesus to promote God's intentions for mankind. It is equally certain it did not happen as is described in John's Gospel. It is not conducive to the sequence of historical events as put together in the Bible, that such an important miracle had happened prior to the crucifixion, but we must not allow this to distract from its importance. God saw an opportunity and took it."

"From the Bible we learn that Lazarus was a close friend of Jesus. They had spent time together. Lazarus was a believer in what Jesus was attempting to do and his sister Mary had washed and anointed the feet of Jesus. He walked everywhere. There was a close bond between them."

"It is written in John's Gospel that Mary wrote to him with the news that her brother Lazarus was very ill. She stated she believed he would recover if Jesus came to see him. Jesus sent a message back saying if Lazarus was ill, that he would recover and that he would visit them in two days. The reason for this delay is not given. Then he received a second message that Lazarus was close to death."

"He immediately set off but when he arrived he found the sisters Martha and Mary in great distress. Lazarus had died and had been entombed for four days. The Bible says there was a stench of decomposition around his tomb. Jesus wept with Mary and the few who were still around to comfort her and he asked if he could be taken to the tomb. The huge stone covering the entrance was rolled away and the helpers stepped back to escape from the smell, as Jesus walked inside to behold his friend."

"His fears were immediately confirmed as he looked at the lifeless body of Lazarus. Feeling distraught he spoke to his Father: "Did I fail my beloved friend Father? Should I have been here? Mary has such strong belief that my presence would have prevented this. What can I possibly say to her to help her in this time of grieving?"

God immediately responded by giving him the power to see the spirit of Lazarus, looking as though it was the real person, standing next to his body. And God said to Jesus: "Tell Mary that Lazarus is risen. Tell her he is now with me."

"Jesus immediately stepped outside, his spirit uplifted with joy, as he said to Martha and Mary: "All is well Mary. Lazarus is risen. He is with my Father."

"There can be no doubt that he would have made absolutely certain that the sisters understood exactly what he was saying. It was a time when kindness, compassion and understanding was not only necessary to help Mary. It was also a time when God knew that Jesus required divine inspiration and assistance to carry on with the work he was doing."

"But the others who had heard what he had said, rejoiced in amazement, and rushed away to tell everyone what they had seen and heard. And almost all of those who had been a witness would have believed that Lazarus was alive and in sound physical health, because that was the custom and what religious people believed and what they would have expected– that those who inherited resurrection, would rise from their graves unaffected by their time in the tomb."

"No further mention of Lazarus appears in the Bible. If he had simply resumed his physical life, it is impossible to think he would not have been at the Cross to be with his great friend during his crucifixion."

Everyone contemplates what was said. Then Ralph adds softly: "I will find where the Apostle John writes about Lazarus so that you can compare the two versions. Then we can talk about it. It is important that you should get it right from your new beginning." He is aware of Raf's wide-eyed expression and waits. Raf's voice is very steady: "I like what Paul said about dying sir…."

Jenny swiftly moves to where he is sitting and kneels down next to him. "We are just beginning to live again Raf. I also like what he said, but we must get things right in our minds and into our lives. I am very happy today. Please be happy with me."

~ ~ ~ ~ ~

The following day St Pauls the Junior witnessed two very rare and very special ceremonies.

A friend of Ralph, an Arch-deacon wearing all the paraphernalia he could muster baptised Jennifer Duncan and Rafael Duncan.

Ralph and his wife acted as godparents.

And shortly after that, with the curtains drawn and the candles lit Travis and Jenny were married with Jonny Singer the best man. Ralph gave the bride away.

And as the groom kissed the bride Raf asked: "How long will it take for Travis to adopt me?" And with everyone looking expectantly at him, his eyes lit up and his lips split into a slow smile.